TEXT BOOK OF PHYSICAL PHARMACEUTICS – 1

[According to latest syllabus of B. Pharm – III semester of Pharmacy Council of India]

Ms. Zankhana Sheth

Associate Professor and Head

Department of Pharmaceutics

Sardar Patel College of Pharmacy,

Sardar Patel Education Campus

managed by Tirupati Foundation

Trust,

Bakrol, Anand (Gujarat)

Mr. Ankur Patel

Assistant Professor

Sardar Patel College of Pharmacy,

Bakrol from Gujarat Technological

University,

Ahmedabad (Gujarat)

Mr. Saurabh Sharma

Assistant Professor

Sardar Patel College of Pharmacy,

Bakrol, Anand (Gujarat)

Ms. Riya Raulji

Assistant Professor

Sardar Patel College of Pharmacy,

Bakrol, Anand (Gujarat)

Ms. Rashika Jain

Assistant Professor

Sardar Patel College of Pharmacy,

Bakrol, Anand (Gujarat)

Mr. Shreykumar H. Patel

Assistant Professor

Sardar Patel College of Pharmacy,

Bakrol, from Gujarat Technological

University,

Ahmedabad (Gujarat)

NOTION PRESS

TEXT BOOK OF

PHYSICAL PHARMACEUTICS – 1

First Edition 2024

Published by:

NOTION PRESS
Publisher and distributor
Head office: Notion press Media Pvt. Ltd.
7, Red cross Road,
Egmore, Chennai,Tamil Nadu 60008

E-mail publish@notionpress.com
Website: www.notionpress.com

TEXT BOOK OF PHYSICAL PHARMACEUTICS – 1
NOTION PRESS
PREFACE

The authors feel great pleasure in presenting the first edition of the book **"Text Book of Physical Pharmaceutics – I"** for graduate students. The present book on **Text Book of Physical Pharmaceutics – 1** has been written according to the syllabus of B. Pharm - III semester of Pharmacy Council of India and covers full course of the subject.

THE SALIENT FEATURES OF THE BOOK ARE: -

- *Easy to understand style of writing* which makes the book a self-study material.

- *Each new concept has been introduced through day-today problem of interest* to the students which makes the subject matter interesting.

- *The language of the book, on the whole, is lucid and easy to understand.*

- Wherever needed *neatly labeled figures have been drawn.*

The authors hope that the students, teachers and other readers will find the book interesting and to the point covering the course. We hope that the students will receive the book warmly.

I express a sincere thank you to the Management of Department of Pharmaceutics, Sardar Patel College of Pharmacy, Sardar Patel Education Campus managed by Tirupati Foundation Trust, and Sardar Patel College of Pharmacy for their support during the writing of this book.

Every effort is made to keep the book error free. The author will gratefully acknowledge the suggestions to improve the book to make it more useful.

Wishing our readers success in examination and life ahead. The authors feel that their efforts will be fully rewarded if the book serves the purpose for which it is written.

CONTENTS

CHAPTER – 1

SOLUBILITY OF DRUGS

INTRODUCTION:

The solubility of drugs is a critical aspect of pharmacology and pharmaceutical sciences. It refers to the ability of a drug compound to dissolve in a solvent, typically water or other physiological fluids. Understanding drug solubility is essential for drug formulation, delivery, and efficacy. Here's a detailed introduction to the solubility of drugs:

Importance of Drug Solubility:

1. **Bioavailability**: Solubility influences how efficiently a drug is absorbed into the bloodstream after administration. Poorly soluble drugs may have lower bioavailability, leading to reduced therapeutic effects.

2. **Formulation Development**: Solubility data guides the selection of appropriate excipients and formulation techniques to improve drug solubility and stability.

3. **Dosage Form Design**: Solubility determines the type of dosage forms that can be developed, such as tablets, capsules, suspensions, or solutions.

4. **Drug Delivery Systems**: Solubility affects the design of drug delivery systems like nanoparticles, liposomes, and micelles, which can enhance solubility and target drug delivery to specific tissues.

Factors Affecting Drug Solubility:

1. **Chemical Structure**: Molecular properties such as polarity, hydrogen bonding, and stereochemistry influence drug solubility. Polar and hydrophilic compounds tend to be more soluble in water, while nonpolar and hydrophobic compounds are more soluble in organic solvents.

2. **pH**: The pH of the solution can significantly affect drug solubility, especially for weak acids and bases. Many drugs exhibit pH-dependent solubility due to ionization effects.

3. **Temperature**: Generally, solubility increases with temperature for most solids dissolving in liquids. However, this relationship may vary depending on the specific drug and solvent system.

4. **Particle Size:** Finely divided particles have a higher surface area, leading to increased solubility due to better exposure to the solvent.

5. **Salt Formation**: Converting a drug into its salt form can enhance solubility by altering its physicochemical properties.

6. **Solvent Selection**: Different drugs may exhibit varying solubilities in different solvents. Choosing the appropriate solvent for a specific drug is crucial for formulation development.

Methods for Determining Drug Solubility:

1. **Shake Flask Method**: A common laboratory technique involves adding excess drug to a solvent, agitating the mixture, and then measuring the concentration of dissolved drug using analytical methods such as UV-Vis spectroscopy or HPLC.

2. **Thermodynamic Solubility Studies**: These studies involve measuring the equilibrium solubility of a drug at different temperatures to determine its thermodynamic solubility profile.

3. **pH-Solubility Profile**: Determining the solubility of a drug at different pH values can provide insights into its ionization behavior and help optimize formulation pH.

4. **Kinetic Solubility Studies**: These studies assess the rate at which a drug dissolves in a solvent, providing information on dissolution kinetics and potential precipitation issues.

Applications of Drug Solubility Data:

1. **Formulation Optimization**: Solubility data is used to optimize drug formulations for improved stability, bioavailability, and patient compliance.

2. **Predicting In Vivo Performance**: In silico modeling techniques utilize drug solubility data to predict in vivo behavior and guide drug development decisions.

3. **Quality Control**: Solubility data is an essential parameter for quality control during drug manufacturing to ensure consistency and efficacy of the final product.

4. **Regulatory Requirements**: Regulatory agencies often require solubility data as part of drug development submissions to assess safety and efficacy.

SOLUBILITY EXPRESSIONS

In the context of drug solubility, solubility expressions are mathematical representations used to quantify the solubility of a drug compound in a given solvent. These expressions provide valuable insights into the relationship between solute concentration and various factors affecting solubility. Here are some common solubility expressions used in pharmaceutical sciences:

Solubility Product (Ksp):

The solubility product (Ksp) is a thermodynamic constant representing the equilibrium solubility of a sparingly soluble salt in a solvent. It is defined as the product of the ion concentrations raised to their stoichiometric coefficients in the equilibrium equation for dissolution. The expression for Ksp is given as:

$$Ksp = [A+]m \times [B-]n$$

Where:

A+B− are the ions of the salt. m and n are the stoichiometric coefficients of the ions.

Henry's Law Constant (H):

Henry's Law describes the solubility of a gas in a liquid solvent at a constant temperature. The Henry's Law constant (H) represents the proportionality between the partial pressure of the gas above the solution and its concentration in the solution. The expression for Henry's Law is given as:

$$C = k_H \cdot P$$

Where:

C is the concentration of the gas in the liquid (typically in moles per liter, M).

- k_H is the Henry's Law constant (specific to each gas-liquid combination, usually given in units of M/atm or similar).

- P is the partial pressure of the gas above the liquid (typically in atmospheres, atm).

Example Calculation

Suppose the Henry's Law constant for CO_2 in water at 25°C is 3.3×10^{-2} M/atm. If the partial pressure of CO_2 above the water is 2 atm, the concentration of dissolved CO_2 in the water can be calculated as:

$$C = k_H \cdot P$$
$$C = (3.3 \times 10^{-2}\,\text{M/atm}) \times (2\,\text{atm})$$
$$C = 6.6 \times 10^{-2}\,\text{M}$$

Therefore, the concentration of CO_2 in the water would be 0.066 M.

Ostwald's Solubility Coefficient (L):

Ostwald's solubility coefficient (L) is used to express the solubility of a gas in a liquid solvent under specific conditions, typically at a particular temperature and pressure. It represents the ratio of the concentration of the dissolved gas to its partial pressure in the gas phase. The expression for Ostwald's solubility coefficient is given as:

Mathematically:

$$L = \frac{V_{dissolved}}{V_{gas}}$$

where:

- $V_{dissolved}$ is the volume of the gas dissolved in the liquid.
- V_{gas} is the volume of the gas in the gas phase under the same conditions of temperature and pressure.

Applications of Henry's Law

1. Carbonated Beverages: The fizz in carbonated drinks is due to carbon dioxide (CO_2)) dissolved under high pressure. When the bottle or can is opened, the pressure decreases, and CO_2 escapes, forming bubbles.
2. Scuba Diving: Divers need to be aware of the solubility of gases like nitrogen in blood at high pressures. Rapid ascent can cause dissolved nitrogen to come out of solution quickly, leading to decompression sickness ("the bends").
3. Environmental Science: Henry's Law helps understand the dissolution of gases such as oxygen and carbon dioxide in bodies of water, which is crucial for aquatic life and processes like photosynthesis and respiration.
4. Pharmaceuticals: The solubility of gases in liquids is important for the manufacture and storage of certain drugs, especially those administered as gases or aerosols.

Factors Affecting Henry's Law

- Temperature: The solubility of gases in liquids generally decreases with increasing temperature. Thus, k_H can be temperature-dependent.
- Nature of the Gas and Liquid: Different gases and liquids have different interactions, leading to different values of k_H

Nernst Distribution Law:

The Nernst distribution law describes the distribution of a solute between two immiscible solvents in equilibrium. It is expressed as the ratio of the concentrations of the solute in each solvent phase and is given by:

The Nernst Distribution Law can be mathematically expressed as:

$$K_D = \frac{C_1}{C_2}$$

where:

- K_D is the distribution coefficient (or partition coefficient).
- C_1 is the concentration of the solute in solvent 1.
- C_2 is the concentration of the solute in solvent 2.

Assumptions

1. Immiscibility of Solvents: The two solvents are immiscible or nearly immiscible, meaning they do not mix significantly.
2. Dilute Solutions: The solute concentrations are sufficiently low so that the solutions can be considered ideal.
3. Constant Temperature: The temperature remains constant during the distribution process.

Applications of Nernst Distribution Law

1. Extraction Processes: Used in the separation of compounds based on their differing solubilities in two solvents.
2. Chromatography: Basis for the separation of components in a mixture in various chromatographic techniques.
3. Pharmaceuticals: Understanding drug distribution between aqueous and lipid phases, which is crucial for drug formulation and delivery.
4. Environmental Science: Analyzing the distribution of pollutants between water and organic phases.

Factors Affecting the Distribution Coefficient

1. Nature of Solvent and Solute: Different chemical properties can significantly influence solubility and, therefore, the distribution coefficient.

2. Temperature: The distribution coefficient is temperature-dependent, as solubility can vary with temperature.

3. Ionic Strength and pH: For ionic solutes, changes in ionic strength and pH of the aqueous phase can affect the distribution.

Limitations

1. Non-Ideal Behavior: At higher concentrations, deviations from ideal behavior can occur.

2. Chemical Reactions: If the solute undergoes chemical reactions in either solvent, the simple distribution law may not apply.

3. Complex Formation: Interaction of the solute with other species in the solvent can alter the distribution ratio.

Henderson-Hasselbalch Equation:

The Henderson-Hasselbalch equation is used to calculate the pH-dependent solubility of weak acids and bases. It relates the pH of a solution to the pKa (acid dissociation constant) of the solute and the ratio of its ionized and unionized forms. The equation is given as:

For a weak acid (HA) that dissociates into its conjugate base (A^-) and a proton (H^+), the Henderson-Hasselbalch equation is given by:

$$pH = pKa + \log\left(\frac{[A^-]}{[HA]}\right)$$

where:

- pH is the measure of acidity of the solution.

- pKa is the negative base-10 logarithm of the acid dissociation constant (Ka) of the acid.

- $[A^-]$ is the concentration of the conjugate base.

- $[HA]$ is the concentration of the weak acid.

Derivation of the Henderson-Hasselbalch Equation

The equation is derived from the expression for the acid dissociation constant Ka:

$$Ka = \frac{[H^+][A^-]}{[HA]}$$

Taking the negative logarithm of both sides:

$$-\log(Ka) = -\log\left(\frac{[H^+][A^-]}{[HA]}\right)$$

This simplifies to:

$$pKa = \log\left(\frac{[HA]}{[H^+][A^-]}\right)$$

Rearranging and solving for pH:

$$pH = \log\left(\frac{1}{[H^+]}\right) = -\log([H^+])$$

Then substituting back, we get:

$$pH = pKa + \log\left(\frac{[A^-]}{[HA]}\right)$$

$\downarrow$

Applications of the Henderson-Hasselbalch Equation

1. Buffer Solutions: Used to design buffer solutions with a desired pH by selecting appropriate acid-conjugate base pairs.
2. Biological Systems: Helps in understanding and controlling the pH of biological systems, such as blood, where bicarbonate acts as a buffer.
3. Pharmaceuticals: Assists in the formulation of drugs that need to maintain a specific pH for stability and activity.
4. Environmental Science: Useful in studying the pH of natural waters and soil chemistry.

Limitations

1. Strong Acids/Bases: The equation is less accurate for solutions of strong acids or bases, which fully dissociate in solution.
2. High Concentrations: At very high concentrations, interactions between ions can cause deviations from ideal behavior.
3. Dilute Solutions: Extremely dilute solutions may also not follow the equation perfectly due to water's own ionization becoming significant.

MECHANISMS OF SOLUTE SOLVENT INTERACTIONS

Understanding the mechanisms of solute-solvent interactions is crucial for comprehending drug solubility behavior. These interactions dictate how drug molecules interact with solvent molecules, influencing their dissolution and solubility characteristics. Here are the main mechanisms of solute-solvent interactions in the context of drug solubility:

1. Hydration/Solvation:

a. **Hydrogen Bonding**: Many drug molecules contain hydrogen bond donor or acceptor groups (e.g., hydroxyl, amino, and carbonyl groups) that can interact with solvent molecules through hydrogen bonding. Water, being a highly polar solvent, can form hydrogen bonds with such functional groups, facilitating drug dissolution.

b. **Dipole-Dipole Interactions**: Polar drug molecules interact with solvent molecules through dipole-dipole interactions. These interactions occur between the partial positive and negative charges of polar molecules, leading to solvation and dissolution of the drug in the solvent.

2. Ion-Dipole Interactions:

a. **Ionization**: Drugs that ionize in solution interact with solvent molecules through ion-dipole interactions. For example, weak acids or bases dissociate into ions in aqueous solutions, and the resulting ions are solvated by surrounding water molecules through electrostatic interactions.

b. **Solubility of Ionic Compounds**: Ionic drug compounds dissolve in solvents through interactions between ions and solvent molecules. The solvation of ions stabilizes the ions in solution, leading to increased solubility.

3. Nonpolar Interactions:

a. **Hydrophobic Effect**: Nonpolar drug molecules interact with nonpolar regions of solvent molecules (e.g., hydrocarbon tails in micelles) through hydrophobic interactions. These interactions are driven by the tendency of nonpolar molecules to minimize contact with polar solvent molecules, leading to solubilization of nonpolar drugs in nonpolar solvents.

b. **Dispersion Forces**: Dispersion forces, also known as London dispersion forces, arise due to temporary fluctuations in electron distribution within molecules. Even nonpolar molecules can interact with each other through these weak forces, contributing to their solvation in nonpolar solvents.

4. Complexation:

Host-Guest Interactions: Some drugs can form complexes with solvent molecules or other substances present in the solvent. For example, cyclodextrins can form inclusion complexes with hydrophobic drug molecules, enhancing their solubility by encapsulating them within their hydrophobic cavities.

5. Particle Size Effects:

Surface Interactions: Finely divided drug particles have a higher surface area available for interactions with solvent molecules. This increased surface area enhances solute-solvent interactions, leading to improved dissolution rates and solubility.

6. pH-Dependent Interactions:

Ionization Equilibrium: For weak acids and bases, the degree of ionization is pH-dependent. Changes in pH can affect the solubility of such drugs by altering their ionization equilibrium and the resulting solute-solvent interactions.

IDEAL SOLUBILITY PARAMETERS

The concept of ideal solubility parameters is rooted in the theory that compounds with similar solubility parameters are more likely to dissolve in one another. In the context of drug solubility, understanding ideal solubility parameters can aid in predicting the compatibility of drugs with specific solvents or excipients, thus facilitating formulation development. Here's a detailed exploration of ideal solubility parameters in the solubility of drugs:

1. Hansen Solubility Parameters (HSP):

Hansen solubility parameters provide a quantitative approach to characterize the solubility behavior of materials, including drugs, based on their three main components:

a. **Dispersion Force Interaction Parameter (δd):** Reflects the ability of a substance to interact through van der Waals forces.

b. **Polar Force Interaction Parameter (δp):** Represents the ability of a substance to interact through dipole-dipole interactions.

c. **Hydrogen Bonding Force Interaction Parameter (δh):** Indicates the ability of a substance to interact through hydrogen bonding.

Matching the solubility parameters of drugs with those of solvents or excipients can predict compatibility and solubility. Ideally, substances with similar solubility parameters are expected to dissolve well together.

2. Flory-Huggins Theory:

The Flory-Huggins theory describes the thermodynamics of mixing in polymer solutions but can also be applied to drug-solvent interactions. According to this theory, the solubility of a drug in a solvent is influenced by the entropy of mixing and the interaction parameter (χ) between the drug and the solvent.

a. **Entropy of Mixing**: Higher entropy of mixing favors solubility. It suggests that a solvent that disrupts the molecular order of the drug will enhance solubility.

b. **Interaction Parameter (χ)**: Reflects the strength and type of interactions between drug molecules and solvent molecules. A positive value of χ indicates favorable interactions, while a negative value indicates unfavorable interactions.

3. Hildebrand Solubility Parameter:

The Hildebrand solubility parameter provides a simplified approach to estimate solubility based on the cohesive energy density of a substance. It does not differentiate between different types of intermolecular interactions but gives a general idea of solubility compatibility.

Matching the Hildebrand solubility parameters of drugs and solvents can provide insights into their solubility behavior. However, it may not account for specific interactions such as hydrogen bonding or dipole-dipole interactions.

4. Kawakita Equation:

The Kawakita equation is another approach used to predict drug solubility by considering the solubility parameter of the solvent and the drug's molar volume. It assumes that solubility is determined by the balance between drug-solvent interactions and the available space in the solvent for drug molecules.

SOLVATION & ASSOCIATION

Solvation and association are two fundamental processes that occur when drug molecules dissolve in a solvent. Understanding these processes is crucial for elucidating the solubility behavior of drugs and designing effective drug formulations. Let's delve into solvation and association in the context of drug solubility:

1. Solvation:

Solvation refers to the process by which solvent molecules surround and interact with solute molecules (such as drug molecules), leading to their dispersion and stabilization in the solvent. This process is driven by various intermolecular forces, including:

a. **Hydrogen Bonding**: Solvent molecules with hydrogen bond donor or acceptor groups can form hydrogen bonds with functional groups present in drug molecules, facilitating their solvation. Water, being a highly polar solvent, is especially effective in solvating polar and hydrophilic drug molecules.

b. **Dipole-Dipole Interactions**: Polar drug molecules interact with solvent molecules through dipole-dipole interactions. Solvent molecules align themselves around the solute molecule, with the partially positive end of one solvent molecule attracted to the partially negative end of another, stabilizing the solute-solvent complex.

c. **Ion-Dipole Interactions**: Ionic drug molecules interact with solvent molecules through ion-dipole interactions. Solvent molecules surround and solvate the ions, stabilizing them in solution through electrostatic interactions.

d. **Hydration**: In aqueous solutions, solvation of drug molecules by water molecules is termed hydration. Water molecules form hydration shells around the solute molecules, effectively dissolving and stabilizing them in solution.

2. Association:

Association refers to the tendency of molecules to associate or form aggregates in solution, often through noncovalent interactions such as hydrogen bonding or hydrophobic interactions. In the context of drug solubility, association can influence the solubility behavior of drugs in several ways:

a. **Micelle Formation**: Amphiphilic drug molecules with both hydrophobic and hydrophilic regions may associate to form micelles in solution. This is particularly relevant for drugs with surfactant properties or those formulated in micellar drug delivery systems. Micelle formation can enhance the solubility of hydrophobic drug molecules by encapsulating them within the hydrophobic core of the micelle, thereby improving their solubility and bioavailability.

b. **Complexation**: Drug molecules may associate with other molecules or ions present in the solution to form complexes. For example, cyclodextrins can form inclusion complexes with hydrophobic drug molecules, enhancing their solubility by encapsulating them within their hydrophobic cavities.

QUANTITATIVE APPROACH TO THE FACTORS INFLUENCING SOLUBILITY OF DRUGS

A quantitative approach to understanding the factors influencing the solubility of drugs involves analyzing various physicochemical properties and parameters that govern solubility behavior. By quantitatively assessing these factors, scientists can predict and optimize drug solubility, thereby facilitating drug development and formulation design. Here's a detailed exploration of the quantitative approach to factors influencing the solubility of drugs:

1. Chemical Structure Analysis:

a. **Molecular Weight**: Generally, smaller molecules tend to have higher solubility due to their greater surface area-to-volume ratio, facilitating interactions with solvent molecules.

b. **Functional Groups**: The presence of polar functional groups (e.g., hydroxyl, amino, carboxyl) enhances solubility through hydrogen bonding and dipole-dipole interactions. Conversely, nonpolar functional groups decrease solubility.

c. **Ionization Constants (pKa):** The ionization behavior of acidic or basic functional groups influences solubility, especially in pH-dependent solubility systems.

2. Thermodynamic Parameters:

a. **Solubility Product (Ksp):** The equilibrium solubility of sparingly soluble salts in a solvent is governed by the solubility product constant, which depends on the concentration of ions in solution.

b. **Henry's Law Constant (H):** Describes the solubility of gases in liquids at a constant temperature and pressure. It quantifies the relationship between gas concentration and partial pressure.

3. Physical Properties:

a. **Melting Point:** Generally, compounds with lower melting points tend to have higher solubility, as they require less energy to overcome intermolecular forces and enter the solvent phase.

b. **Particle Size and Surface Area:** Fine particle size increases surface area and enhances solubility by providing more sites for solvent interaction. This relationship is described by the Noyes-Whitney equation.

4. Solvent-Solute Interactions:

a. **Hansen Solubility Parameters:** Quantitatively describe solute-solvent interactions based on dispersion, polar, and hydrogen bonding forces. Matching solubility parameters can predict solubility behavior.

b. **Flory-Huggins Interaction Parameter (χ):** Quantifies the strength and type of interactions between drug and solvent molecules. Positive values indicate favorable interactions, while negative values indicate unfavorable interactions.

5. Kinetic Factors:

a. **Dissolution Rate Constants:** Describe the rate at which a solid drug dissolves in a solvent. Higher dissolution rates typically lead to faster onset of action and improved bioavailability.

b. **Particle Dissolution Rate:** Affected by factors such as agitation, temperature, and particle size distribution.

6. pH-Dependent Solubility:

Henderson-Hasselbalch Equation: Quantifies the pH-dependent solubility of weak acids and bases based on their pKa values and the pH of the solution.

DIFFUSION PRINCIPLES IN BIOLOGICAL SYSTEMS

Diffusion principles play a fundamental role in understanding the transport and distribution of drugs within biological systems, particularly regarding drug solubility. Here's an in-depth exploration of diffusion principles in biological systems as they relate to the solubility of drugs:

1. Fick's First Law of Diffusion:

Fick's first law describes the rate of diffusion of a solute across a concentration gradient within a homogeneous medium. In the context of drug solubility:

$J = -D\frac{dC}{dx}$

J: Diffusion flux (amount of solute moving through a unit area per unit time).

D: Diffusion coefficient (a measure of how quickly the solute diffuses through the medium).

$\frac{dC}{dx}$: Concentration gradient (change in concentration per unit distance). This law helps quantify the movement of drugs from regions of higher concentration (e.g., drug formulation) to regions of lower concentration (e.g., target tissues) within biological systems.

2. Diffusion in Biological Membranes:

a. **Cell Membranes**: Drugs often need to cross cellular membranes to reach their target sites. Membrane permeability depends on factors such as molecular size, lipophilicity, and the presence of specific transporters. Lipid-soluble drugs diffuse readily through cell membranes, while polar or charged drugs may require transporter-mediated or facilitated diffusion.

b. **Blood-Brain Barrier (BBB)**: The BBB restricts the passage of many drugs from the bloodstream to the brain due to its unique structure composed of tight junctions between endothelial cells. Drugs must be sufficiently lipid-soluble or possess specific transport mechanisms to penetrate the BBB.

3. Diffusion in Biological Fluids:

a. **Blood Plasma**: Drug molecules dissolved in blood plasma undergo diffusion between the bloodstream and tissues. Factors such as protein binding, pH, and blood flow rate influence drug distribution and solubility in plasma.

b. **Interstitial Fluid**: Diffusion through interstitial fluid determines the distribution of drugs within tissues. The rate of diffusion is influenced by factors such as tissue composition, vascular permeability, and molecular size.

4. Factors Influencing Diffusion:

a. **Concentration Gradient**: The driving force for diffusion is the concentration gradient between two regions. Higher concentration gradients lead to faster diffusion rates.

b. **Temperature**: Increasing temperature enhances the kinetic energy of molecules, leading to faster diffusion rates.

c. **Medium Characteristics**: The diffusion coefficient D is influenced by the properties of the medium, such as viscosity and molecular size.

5. Drug Formulation Considerations:

a. **Particle Size**: Nanoparticles and other particulate formulations can enhance drug solubility and diffusion by increasing surface area and reducing diffusion distances.

b. **Hydrophilic/Lipophilic Balance**: Formulating drugs with appropriate hydrophilic/lipophilic balance can influence their solubility and diffusion properties within biological systems.

SOLUBILITY OF GAS IN LIQUIDS OF BINARY SOLUTIONS

The solubility of gases in liquids, particularly within binary solutions, is a crucial aspect of drug formulation and pharmacokinetics, especially for drugs administered via inhalation, injection, or other routes where gas-liquid interactions are significant. Let's delve into the solubility of gases in liquids within binary solutions in detail:

1. Henry's Law:

Henry's Law describes the solubility of a gas in a liquid at a constant temperature. It states that the concentration of a gas dissolved in a liquid is directly proportional to the partial pressure of the gas above the liquid. Mathematically, Henry's Law is expressed as:

$$C = kH \times P$$

Where:

C is the concentration of the gas in the liquid (mol/L).

kH is Henry's Law constant, representing the solubility of the gas in the liquid (mol/L·atm).

P is the partial pressure of the gas above the liquid (atm).

2. Binary Solutions:

In binary solutions, two components are involved: a solvent (usually a liquid) and a solute (gas). The solute gas dissolves in the liquid solvent, forming a homogeneous mixture. The solubility of the gas in the liquid is influenced by various factors, including:

a. **Nature of the Solvent**: The chemical composition and physical properties of the solvent determine its ability to dissolve gases. Polar solvents, such as water, tend to dissolve polar gases more readily due to stronger intermolecular interactions.

b. **Temperature**: Solubility of gases generally decreases with increasing temperature, following Henry's Law. Higher temperatures disrupt the equilibrium between gas molecules in the liquid phase and those in the gas phase, leading to decreased solubility.

c. **Pressure**: According to Henry's Law, the solubility of a gas in a liquid is directly proportional to the partial pressure of the gas above the liquid. Increasing pressure enhances gas solubility in the liquid phase.

3. Applications in Drug Formulation:

a. **Gas Dissolution in Injectable Formulations**: In parenteral drug formulations, such as injectables, understanding the solubility of gases in the liquid phase is crucial for preventing gas bubble formation, which can lead to embolism or stability issues.

b. **Inhalation Therapy**: For inhalable drugs delivered via nebulizers or metered-dose inhalers (MDIs), gas solubility in the liquid formulation affects drug delivery efficiency and particle size distribution, impacting therapeutic efficacy.

c. **Solvent Selection**: Solvent choice in drug formulations can significantly influence gas solubility and stability. Selecting appropriate solvents with desired gas solubility characteristics is essential for formulating safe and effective drug products.

SOLUBILITY OF GAS IN LIQUIDS OF IDEAL SOLUTIONS

In the context of drug solubility, the solubility of gases in liquids within ideal solutions provides a theoretical framework for understanding the behavior of gases dissolved in liquid solvents. Let's explore the solubility of gases in liquids within ideal solutions in detail:

1. Ideal Solution Theory:

In an ideal solution, interactions between solvent molecules and solute molecules (gas in this case) are assumed to be negligible, meaning there are no intermolecular forces between solute molecules or between solute and solvent molecules. Ideal solutions serve as a theoretical model to simplify the analysis of solute-solvent interactions.

2. Henry's Law in Ideal Solutions:

Henry's Law, which describes the solubility of gases in liquids, can be applied to ideal solutions. According to Henry's Law, the concentration of a gas dissolved in a liquid is directly proportional to the partial pressure of the gas above the liquid. In an ideal solution, Henry's Law is expressed as:

$C=kH\times P$

Where:

C is the concentration of the gas in the liquid.

kH is Henry's Law constant, representing the solubility of the gas in the liquid.

P is the partial pressure of the gas above the liquid.

In an ideal solution, Henry's Law holds true over a wide range of concentrations and pressures.

3. Characteristics of Ideal Solutions:

a. **Non-Interacting Components**: The solute (gas) and solvent molecules do not interact with each other or with themselves, simplifying calculations of solubility and solution properties.

b. **Raoult's Law**: Raoult's Law, which describes the vapor pressure of ideal solutions, can also be applied to gas solubility in liquids. According to Raoult's Law, the partial pressure of each component in the vapor phase is directly proportional to its mole fraction in the liquid phase.

c. **Ideal Gas Behavior**: The solute gas is assumed to behave as an ideal gas, meaning its behavior conforms to the ideal gas law.

4. Applications in Drug Formulation:

a. **Theoretical Model**: Ideal solutions serve as a theoretical model for understanding gas solubility in liquid solvents. While real-world solutions may deviate from ideality due to interactions between solute and solvent molecules, ideal solution theory provides a useful framework for analysis.

b. **Predictive Tool**: Ideal solution theory can be used to predict the behavior of gases in liquid solvents under various conditions of temperature, pressure, and concentration.

SOLUBILITY OF LIQUIDS IN LIQUIDS OF BINARY SOLUTIONS

The solubility of liquids in liquids, particularly within binary solutions, is a critical aspect of drug formulation, especially for drugs administered via oral, topical, or parenteral routes where liquid-liquid interactions are significant. Let's explore the solubility of liquids in liquids within binary solutions in detail:

1. Liquid-Liquid Equilibrium:

In binary liquid solutions, two components are involved: a solvent (typically a liquid) and a solute (another liquid). The solubility of one liquid in another depends on various factors, including:

a. **Chemical Compatibility**: The solute and solvent should be chemically compatible to ensure homogeneous mixing and stability of the solution.

b. **Intermolecular Interactions**: The interactions between molecules of the solute and solvent play a crucial role in determining solubility. These interactions include hydrogen bonding, dipole-dipole interactions, and London dispersion forces.

2. Factors Influencing Solubility:

a. **Polarity:** Polar solvents tend to dissolve polar solutes more readily due to stronger intermolecular interactions. Nonpolar solvents dissolve nonpolar solutes more effectively.

b. **Similarity in Molecular Structure**: Liquids with similar molecular structures and polarities are more likely to be miscible with each other.

c. **Temperature**: Solubility generally increases with temperature for liquid-liquid systems, although this trend may not hold true for all systems.

d. **Pressure**: Unlike gas-liquid systems, pressure has a minimal effect on the solubility of liquids in liquids.

3. Phase Diagrams:

Phase diagrams provide a graphical representation of the solubility behavior of liquids in liquids as a function of temperature and composition. They typically include regions representing single-phase solutions, two-phase mixtures, and the solubility limit at various temperatures.

4. Applications in Drug Formulation:

    a. **Solvent Selection**: Choosing appropriate solvents for drug formulations is crucial for achieving desired solubility and stability. Solvents with high solubility for the drug component are preferred.

    b. **Formulation Development**: Understanding the solubility of liquids in liquids guides the development of various formulations such as suspensions, emulsions, and solutions. It allows for the optimization of drug delivery systems to enhance drug solubility and bioavailability.

    c. **Extraction and Purification**: Liquid-liquid extraction techniques are used in pharmaceutical processes for the purification and isolation of active pharmaceutical ingredients (APIs) from natural sources or reaction mixtures.

SOLUBILITY OF LIQUIDS IN LIQUIDS OF IDEAL SOLUTIONS

In the context of drug solubility, the solubility of liquids in liquids within ideal solutions provides a theoretical framework for understanding the behavior of liquid solutes in liquid solvents. Let's explore the solubility of liquids in liquids within ideal solutions in detail:

1. Ideal Solution Theory:

In an ideal solution, interactions between solvent molecules and solute molecules (liquid in this case) are assumed to be negligible, meaning there are no intermolecular forces between solute molecules or between solute and solvent molecules. Ideal solutions serve as a theoretical model to simplify the analysis of solute-solvent interactions.

2. Raoult's Law in Ideal Solutions:

Raoult's Law describes the vapor pressure of an ideal solution as a function of the vapor pressure of each component in the pure state and the mole fraction of each component in the solution. For liquid-liquid solutions, Raoult's Law can be expressed as:

$$PA = PA* \times xA$$
$$PB = PB* \times xB$$

Where:

PA and PB are the vapor pressures of components A and B in the solution.

$PA*$ and $PB*$ are the vapor pressures of pure components A and B, respectively.

xA and xB are the mole fractions of components A and B in the solution.

According to Raoult's Law, the partial vapor pressure of each component in an ideal solution is directly proportional to its mole fraction in the solution.

3. Characteristics of Ideal Solutions:

a. **Non-Interacting Components**: The solute (liquid) and solvent molecules do not interact with each other or with themselves, simplifying calculations of solubility and solution properties.

b. **Raoult's Law:** Raoult's Law holds true for ideal solutions, facilitating the prediction of vapor pressures and solubilities based on component mole fractions.

4. Applications in Drug Formulation:

a. **Theoretical Model**: Ideal solutions serve as a theoretical model for understanding liquid-liquid interactions in drug formulations. While real-world solutions may deviate from ideality due to interactions between solute and solvent molecules, ideal solution theory provides a useful framework for analysis.

b. **Predictive Tool:** Ideal solution theory can be used to predict the behavior of liquid solutes in liquid solvents under various conditions of temperature and composition. This predictive capability aids in the design and optimization of drug formulations for enhanced solubility and stability.

RAOULT'S LAW

Raoult's Law is a fundamental principle in the field of physical chemistry that describes the vapor pressure of an ideal solution as a function of the vapor pressure of each component in its pure state and the mole fraction of each component in the solution. It has significant implications in understanding the solubility behavior of drugs, especially in liquid-liquid systems. Let's delve into an introduction to Raoult's Law in the context of the solubility of drugs:

Understanding Raoult's Law:

1. **Definition:**

    Raoult's Law states that the partial vapor pressure of a component in an ideal solution is directly proportional to its mole fraction in the solution.

2. **Mathematical Representation:**

For a binary solution containing components A and B:

$$PA = PA* \times xA$$
$$PB = PB* \times xB$$

- **Where:**

    PA and PB are the partial vapor pressures of components A and B in the solution.

    $PA*$ and $PB*$ are the vapor pressures of pure components A and B, respectively.

    xA and xB are the mole fractions of components A and B in the solution.

3. **Key Points:**

    a. According to Raoult's Law, if the solution behaves ideally, the vapor pressure of each component is proportional to its mole fraction in the solution.

b. Deviations from Raoult's Law can occur in real solutions due to interactions between solute and solvent molecules, especially when non-ideal behavior is observed.

Application to Drug Solubility:

1. **Solubility in Liquid Solutions:**

   a. Raoult's Law provides a theoretical framework for understanding the solubility of drugs in liquid solvents.

   b. It helps predict the vapor pressures of drug solutions and their components based on their mole fractions, aiding in the design and optimization of drug formulations.

2. **Liquid-Liquid Extraction:**

   a. Raoult's Law is applicable in liquid-liquid extraction processes used in pharmaceutical manufacturing for the purification and isolation of drug compounds from natural sources or reaction mixtures.

3. **Formulation Design:**

   a. Understanding the solubility behavior of drugs in liquid solvents according to Raoult's Law guides the selection of appropriate solvents and formulation components to achieve desired solubility and stability in pharmaceutical formulations.

REAL SOLUTIONS

In the context of drug solubility, understanding real solutions in the context of Raoult's Law provides insights into deviations from ideal behavior and the factors influencing the solubility of drugs in liquid solvents. Let's explore real solutions in Raoult's Law in detail:

1. Real Solutions vs. Ideal Solutions:

a. **Ideal Solutions**: Ideal solutions are theoretical models where interactions between solute and solvent molecules are assumed to be negligible. In ideal solutions, Raoult's Law accurately describes the vapor pressure behavior of components.

b. **Real Solutions**: Real solutions deviate from ideal behavior due to interactions between solute and solvent molecules. These interactions can lead to deviations from Raoult's Law and affect solubility behavior.

2. Deviations from Raoult's Law:

a. **Positive Deviation**: In some cases, the vapor pressure of a component in a solution is higher than predicted by Raoult's Law. This occurs when the interactions between solute and solvent molecules are stronger than those between solvent molecules. Positive deviations are often observed in mixtures where the components are chemically dissimilar or have significant intermolecular forces.

b. **Negative Deviation**: Conversely, negative deviations occur when the vapor pressure of a component in a solution is lower than predicted by Raoult's Law. This typically happens when the interactions between solute and solvent molecules are weaker than those between solvent molecules. Negative deviations are commonly observed in mixtures where the components are chemically similar or have weak intermolecular forces.

3. Causes of Deviations:

a. **Chemical Compatibility**: Chemical interactions between solute and solvent molecules, such as hydrogen bonding, dipole-dipole interactions, or Van der Waals forces, can lead to deviations from Raoult's Law.

b. **Non-Ideal Behavior**: Real solutions may exhibit non-ideal behavior due to factors such as molecular size disparity, asymmetry, or polarizability, which influence the strength of intermolecular interactions.

c. **Solution Composition**: The composition of the solution, including the relative amounts of solute and solvent, can influence deviations from Raoult's Law.

4. Implications for Drug Solubility:

a. **Formulation Design**: Understanding deviations from Raoult's Law is essential for designing drug formulations with optimized solubility and stability. Formulators must consider real solution behavior when selecting solvents and optimizing drug concentrations.

b. **Process Optimization**: Real solution behavior influences various pharmaceutical processes, including extraction, purification, and crystallization. Optimizing these processes requires accounting for deviations from ideal behavior.

PARTIALLY MISCIBLE LIQUIDS

Partially miscible liquids are those that exhibit limited solubility in each other, meaning they do not completely mix to form a single homogeneous phase. In the context of Raoult's Law and drug solubility, understanding the behavior of partially miscible liquids provides insights into solubility limitations and challenges in formulating drug solutions. Let's explore partially miscible liquids in Raoult's Law and their implications for drug solubility in detail:

1. Partial Miscibility and Raoult's Law:

a. **Limited Mixing**: Partially miscible liquids have limited solubility in each other due to differences in polarity, intermolecular forces, or molecular size. When mixed, they may form two distinct phases rather than a single homogeneous solution.

b. **Raoult's Law for Partially Miscible Liquids**: Raoult's Law describes the vapor pressure behavior of ideal solutions. However, it is not directly applicable to partially miscible liquids since these systems do not form homogeneous solutions. As a result, the vapor pressures of the individual components cannot be accurately described by Raoult's Law.

2. Phase Separation:

a. **Liquid-Liquid Equilibrium**: Partially miscible liquids reach a state of equilibrium where two distinct liquid phases coexist. Each phase has its own composition and vapor pressure.

b. **Binodal Curve**: The phase behavior of partially miscible liquids can be represented by a binodal curve on a phase diagram. The binodal curve delineates the compositions at which two phases coexist in equilibrium.

3. Implications for Drug Solubility:

a. **Solubility Limitations**: Partial miscibility imposes limitations on the solubility of drugs in liquid solvents. If the drug is more soluble in one phase than the other, achieving adequate solubility in the desired phase may be challenging.

b. **Formulation Challenges**: Formulating drugs in partially miscible solvent systems requires careful consideration of phase behavior and solubility limitations. Phase separation can lead to formulation instability, inconsistent dosing, and reduced efficacy.

4. Strategies for Overcoming Solubility Challenges:

a. **Cosolvency**: Using cosolvents or surfactants to enhance solubility by promoting dispersion of the drug in both phases or increasing the miscibility of the solvent phases.

b. **Nanoscale Formulations**: Formulating drugs in nanoscale carriers, such as nanoparticles or nanoemulsions, can improve solubility by increasing the surface area for drug dissolution and minimizing phase separation.

CRITICAL SOLUTION TEMPERATURE

The critical solution temperature (CST) is a crucial concept in the context of Raoult's Law and drug solubility, especially in systems where the solubility behavior of the components undergoes a significant change with temperature. Let's explore the critical solution temperature in Raoult's Law and its implications for drug solubility in detail:

1. Definition of Critical Solution Temperature (CST):

a. The critical solution temperature is the temperature at which two immiscible liquids become completely miscible in all proportions to form a single-phase solution. Above this temperature, the two components are fully soluble in each other, while below this temperature, they separate into two distinct phases.

2. Raoult's Law and CST:

a. Raoult's Law describes the vapor pressure behavior of ideal solutions, where the solute and solvent molecules are assumed to be fully miscible in all proportions. However, Raoult's Law is not directly applicable to systems with a critical solution temperature, as it describes the behavior of ideal solutions.

b. Near the critical solution temperature, the vapor pressures of the components may deviate significantly from those predicted by Raoult's Law due to the formation of a single-phase solution.

3. Implications for Drug Solubility:

a. **Temperature-Dependent Solubility**: The solubility of drugs in liquid solvents can exhibit significant temperature dependence, especially near the critical solution temperature. Understanding this temperature dependence is essential for optimizing drug formulations and predicting drug solubility behavior.

b. **Phase Behavior**: The critical solution temperature influences the phase behavior of liquid-liquid systems, impacting drug solubility and formulation stability. Changes in temperature can lead to phase separation or phase transitions, affecting the solubility and bioavailability of drugs.

4. Experimental Determination:

a. The critical solution temperature can be experimentally determined by observing changes in phase behavior, such as turbidity or the disappearance of phase boundaries, as a function of temperature.

b. Techniques such as cloud point determination, turbidimetry, or differential scanning calorimetry (DSC) can be used to identify the critical solution temperature in liquid-liquid systems.

5. Applications in Drug Formulation:

a. **Formulation Optimization**: Understanding the critical solution temperature is crucial for optimizing drug formulations, especially in systems where temperature-dependent solubility behavior is significant.

b. **Stability Considerations**: Knowledge of the critical solution temperature helps in designing stable drug formulations by avoiding temperature conditions that lead to phase separation or precipitation.

APPLICATIONS RAOULT'S LAW

Raoult's Law, while originally formulated to describe the behavior of ideal solutions, finds numerous applications in the field of drug solubility and pharmaceutical sciences. Here are some detailed applications of Raoult's Law in the context of drug solubility:

1. Formulation Design:

a. **Solvent Selection**: Raoult's Law assists in selecting suitable solvents for drug formulations by predicting their solubility behavior. Understanding the interactions between drug molecules and solvents helps in choosing solvents that maximize drug solubility and stability.

b. **Cosolvency**: Raoult's Law guides the selection of cosolvents to enhance drug solubility. By considering the solubility parameters and interactions between components, cosolvent systems can be designed to improve solubility and formulation flexibility.

2. Solubility Prediction:

a. **Temperature Dependence**: Raoult's Law accounts for temperature-dependent changes in drug solubility by predicting how solubility varies with temperature. This information is crucial for designing formulations with stable solubility profiles over a range of temperatures.

b. **Phase Behavior**: Understanding the phase behavior of drug-solvent mixtures using Raoult's Law aids in predicting drug solubility under different conditions. It helps in identifying temperature regimes where phase separation or precipitation may occur, guiding formulation strategies to mitigate these issues.

3. Process Optimization:

a. **Extraction Processes**: Raoult's Law is applied in liquid-liquid extraction processes for isolating and purifying drug compounds from natural sources or reaction mixtures. By understanding the solubility behavior of drugs in different solvents, extraction processes can be optimized to achieve higher yields and purity.

b. **Crystallization**: In crystallization processes, Raoult's Law helps in selecting appropriate solvents and controlling solution conditions to induce crystallization at desired temperatures. By predicting solubility behavior, Raoult's Law aids in optimizing crystallization processes to obtain pure drug crystals with desired properties.

4. Quality Control:

a. **Solubility Testing**: Raoult's Law serves as a basis for conducting solubility testing during drug development and manufacturing. By comparing experimental solubility data with predictions based on Raoult's Law, the quality and consistency of drug formulations can be evaluated, ensuring compliance with regulatory requirements.

5. Predictive Modeling:

Computational Methods: Raoult's Law can be incorporated into computational models to predict drug solubility behavior and optimize formulation designs. By accounting for molecular interactions and thermodynamic parameters, computational models based on Raoult's Law provide valuable insights into drug solubility in complex systems.

DISTRIBUTION LAW

The distribution law, also known as the partition coefficient or distribution coefficient, is a fundamental concept in the field of drug solubility and pharmacokinetics. It describes the distribution of a solute between two immiscible phases, typically a hydrophilic phase (e.g., water) and a lipophilic phase (e.g., organic solvent or biological membrane). Let's delve into an introduction to the distribution law in the context of drug solubility:

1. Definition:

The distribution law states that at equilibrium, the concentration of a solute distributed between two immiscible phases is proportional to its concentration in each phase and is governed by a constant known as the partition coefficient (K or P).

Mathematically, the distribution law can be expressed as:

$$K = \frac{[S]_{lipid}}{[S]_{aqueous}}$$

Where:

    a. $[S]_{lipid}$ is the concentration of the solute in the lipophilic phase.

    b. $[S]_{aqueous}$ is the concentration of the solute in the aqueous phase.

2. Key Points:

a. **Partition Coefficient**: The partition coefficient (K) quantifies the distribution of a solute between two phases. A higher partition coefficient indicates greater solubility in the lipophilic phase relative to the aqueous phase.

b. **Equilibrium Condition**: The distribution of the solute between the two phases reaches equilibrium when the rate of transfer between phases becomes equal, resulting in a constant partition coefficient at a given temperature.

c. **Factors Affecting Partition Coefficient**: The partition coefficient is influenced by factors such as the nature of the solute and solvent, temperature, pH, and the presence of ionizable groups.

3. Applications:

a. **Drug Absorption and Distribution**: The distribution law is crucial in understanding the absorption, distribution, and tissue penetration of drugs in biological systems. It influences the rate and extent of drug distribution across biological membranes and tissues.

b. **Drug Formulation**: Knowledge of the partition coefficient aids in formulating drug products with optimized solubility and bioavailability. Formulators can design formulations that enhance drug absorption and target specific tissues based on partition coefficient considerations.

c. **Toxicology and Environmental Studies**: The distribution law is applicable in toxicology and environmental studies to predict the distribution and fate of chemicals in biological organisms and environmental matrices.

4. Experimental Determination:

a. **Shake Flask Method**: The partition coefficient can be experimentally determined using the shake flask method, where a known amount of solute is equilibrated between two phases, followed by quantification of solute concentrations in each phase.

b. **High-Performance Liquid Chromatography (HPLC)**: HPLC techniques can be employed to measure the partition coefficient by analyzing the distribution of a solute between a stationary phase (e.g., reversed-phase column) and a mobile phase.

Limitations of Distribution Law

While the distribution law provides valuable insights into the distribution behavior of solutes between two immiscible phases, it also has several limitations that need to be considered when applying it to drug solubility and pharmacokinetics. Let's explore the limitations of the distribution law in detail:

1. Non-Ideal Systems:

a. **Deviation from Ideal Behavior**: The distribution law assumes ideal behavior, where the solute distributes proportionally between the two phases. However, real systems often deviate from ideal behavior due to factors such as solute-solvent interactions, ionization, and complex phase equilibria.

b. **Nonlinear Partitioning**: In non-ideal systems, the partition coefficient may not remain constant across different concentrations or conditions. Nonlinear partitioning can occur due to changes in solute-solvent interactions or phase composition, leading to inaccurate predictions based on the distribution law.

2. Temperature Dependence:

a. **Temperature Effects**: The partition coefficient is often temperature-dependent, with changes in temperature influencing solute solubility and distribution behavior. The distribution law does not account for temperature effects, leading to inaccuracies in predicting solute distribution at different temperatures.

b. **Critical Solution Temperature**: Systems with critical solution temperatures exhibit phase transitions and significant changes in solubility behavior near the critical temperature. The distribution law may not accurately describe solute distribution behavior in such systems.

3. pH and Ionization:

a. **Ionization Effects**: Ionizable solutes can exist in different charged forms depending on the pH of the solution. The distribution law does not account for changes in solute ionization and may provide inaccurate predictions for ionizable compounds, especially in systems with pH gradients.

b. **Ion Pairing**: In some cases, ionizable solutes may form ion pairs or complexes with counterions, affecting their distribution behavior. The distribution law may not accurately predict the distribution of solutes involved in ion-pairing interactions.

4. Solvent Systems:

a. **Limited Applicability**: The distribution law is primarily applicable to systems with two immiscible phases, typically a hydrophilic phase (e.g., water) and a lipophilic phase (e.g., organic solvent). It may not be directly applicable to more complex solvent systems or biological matrices.

b. **Multicomponent Systems**: Systems containing multiple solutes or solvents may exhibit complex interactions and phase behavior that cannot be adequately described by the distribution law alone. Additional factors such as synergistic or antagonistic effects may influence solute distribution in such systems.

Applications of Distribution Law

The distribution law, also known as the partition coefficient or partition law, plays a crucial role in various aspects of drug solubility, pharmacokinetics, and pharmaceutical sciences. Here are detailed applications of the distribution law in the context of drug solubility:

1. Drug Formulation Design:

a. **Solvent Selection**: The distribution law guides the selection of solvents for drug formulations by predicting the solubility behavior of drugs in different solvent systems. Formulators can choose solvents with appropriate partition coefficients to optimize drug solubility and stability.

b. **Cosolvency**: Understanding the partition coefficient assists in designing cosolvent systems to enhance drug solubility. By selecting cosolvents with complementary partition coefficients, formulators can improve drug solubility and overcome formulation challenges.

2. Pharmacokinetics:

a. **Absorption:** The distribution law influences drug absorption by determining the extent to which drugs partition into biological membranes or tissues. Drugs with higher partition coefficients are more likely to penetrate lipid-rich barriers, leading to increased absorption and bioavailability.

b. **Distribution:** Knowledge of the partition coefficient aids in predicting drug distribution within the body. Drugs with high lipid solubility (high partition coefficient) tend to distribute into adipose tissue and cross the blood-brain barrier more readily, affecting their pharmacological effects and distribution kinetics.

3. Toxicology and Environmental Studies:

a. **Bioaccumulation**: The distribution law is applicable in toxicology and environmental studies to predict the bioaccumulation of chemicals in living organisms. Compounds with high partition coefficients may accumulate in fatty tissues and biomagnify in food chains, posing risks to human health and the environment.

b. **Environmental Fate**: Understanding the partition coefficient helps predict the fate and transport of chemicals in environmental matrices. It aids in assessing the potential for environmental contamination, evaluating remediation strategies, and estimating environmental risks associated with chemical exposure.

4. Analytical Chemistry:

a. **Extraction Techniques**: The distribution law is used in extraction techniques such as liquid-liquid extraction and solid-phase extraction to isolate and concentrate analytes from complex matrices. By optimizing extraction conditions based on partition coefficients, analysts can achieve higher extraction efficiencies and sensitivity.

b. **Chromatographic Separations**: In chromatography, the distribution law governs the partitioning of analytes between the stationary and mobile phases. Understanding partition coefficients helps in selecting appropriate chromatographic conditions to achieve efficient separations and detect analytes of interest.

5. Drug Delivery Systems:

Lipid-Based Formulations: Lipid-based drug delivery systems leverage the distribution law to enhance drug solubility and bioavailability. By formulating drugs in lipidic carriers, formulators can increase drug partitioning into lipid-rich environments, leading to improved absorption and therapeutic outcomes.

Multiple Choice Questions (MCQs)

1. What does drug solubility primarily influence in pharmacology?

   A) Drug color

   B) Drug shape

   C) Drug bioavailability

   D) Drug packaging

2. Which method is commonly used for determining drug solubility?

   A) Shake Flask Method

   B) Boiling Point Method

   C) Freezing Point Method

   D) Sublimation Method

3. What effect does pH have on drug solubility?

   A) No effect

   B) Decreases solubility for all drugs

   C) Increases solubility for all drugs

   D) Influences solubility especially for weak acids and bases

4. How does temperature generally affect the solubility of solid drugs in liquids?

   A) Increases solubility

B) Decreases solubility

C) No impact

D) Makes it unpredictable

5. Which of the following is a factor affecting drug solubility?

    A) Color of the drug

    B) Shape of the drug

    C) Particle size of the drug

    D) Price of the drug

6. What does Henry's Law describe?

    A) Solubility of gases in solids

    B) Solubility of solids in liquids

    C) Solubility of gases in liquids

    D) Solubility of liquids in gases

7. The Henderson-Hasselbalch equation is used to calculate:

    A) Reaction rates

    B) pH-dependent solubility

    C) Boiling points

    D) Freezing points

8. Which interaction is not typically involved in solvation processes for drugs?

    A) Hydrogen bonding

    B) Dipole-dipole interactions

    C) Ionic bonding

    D) Covalent bonding

9. What role does the particle size play in drug solubility?

    A) Smaller particles decrease solubility

    B) Larger particles increase solubility

    C) Smaller particles increase solubility

    D) Particle size has no effect

10. Which statement is true about the solubility product (Ksp)?

A) It decreases with increasing solubility

B) It is unrelated to solubility

C) It represents the maximum solubility of a compound

D) It is only relevant for gases

11. Which parameter is NOT part of the Hansen Solubility Parameters?

A) Dispersion force interaction parameter (δd)

B) Polar force interaction parameter (δp)

C) Volume interaction parameter (δv)

D) Hydrogen bonding force interaction parameter (δh)

12. The Flory-Huggins theory is used to describe the solubility in terms of:

A) Entropy of mixing and interaction parameter

B) Melting points and boiling points

C) Molecular weights and densities

D) Viscosity and surface tension

13. What does the Nernst Distribution Law describe?

A) The solubility of a solute between two non-miscible solvents

B) The rate of solute dissolution

C) The temperature dependence of solubility

D) The pH effect on solubility

14. Ion-dipole interactions are particularly important for which type of drugs?

A) Nonpolar drugs

B) Polar drugs

C) Volatile drugs

D) Solid drugs

15. What is the primary application of solubility data in pharmaceuticals?

A) Enhancing the color and taste of drug products

B) Drug packaging

C) Optimizing drug formulations

D) Advertising

16. Which study provides information on how fast a drug dissolves in a solvent?

   A) Shake Flask Method

   B) Thermodynamic Solubility Studies

   C) Kinetic Solubility Studies

   D) pH-Solubility Profile

17. What is the critical solution temperature (CST)?

   A) Temperature at which a solution freeze

   B) Temperature at which a solution boil

   C) Temperature at which two immiscible liquids become completely miscible

   D) Temperature at which a solid dissolve in a liquid

18. What does Raoult's Law relate to in solutions?

   A) pH of the solution

   B) Vapor pressure of the components

   C) Electrical conductivity

   D) Viscosity

19. What is meant by "partition coefficient" in the context of drug solubility?

   A) The ratio of solubility of a drug in water to its solubility in oil

   B) The concentration of a drug in plasma

   C) The rate of drug absorption

   D) The stability of a drug in solution

20. What does the shake flask method measure?

   A) Viscosity of a solution

   B) Concentration of dissolved drug

   C) Temperature stability of a drug

   D) pH of a drug solution

Short Answer Type Questions (Subjective)

1. What is the significance of drug solubility in pharmaceutical sciences?

2. How does solubility influence the bioavailability of drugs?

3. Describe how solubility affects the design of drug delivery systems.

4. What is the role of chemical structure in determining drug solubility?

5. Explain how pH affects the solubility of weak acids and bases.

6. How does temperature generally affect the solubility of solid drugs?

7. What is the Shake Flask Method and what does it measure?

8. Define the solubility product (Ksp) and its importance in pharmaceutical sciences.

9. What is Henry's Law and how does it apply to the solubility of gases?

10. Describe the principle of the Nernst Distribution Law in solubility.

11. How do ion-dipole interactions affect drug solubility?

12. What is meant by the term "complexation" in the context of solubility?

13. Explain the concept of cosolvency in pharmaceutical formulations.

14. What are Hansen Solubility Parameters and how are they used in drug formulation?

15. Define Raoult's Law and its application in drug solubility.

16. How does the critical solution temperature affect drug solubility?

17. Describe how the partition coefficient influences drug absorption and distribution.

18. What is the relevance of liquid-liquid extraction in pharmaceutical manufacturing?

19. How does the distribution law apply to the environmental fate of chemicals?

20. Explain how lipid-based formulations utilize the distribution law to enhance drug bioavailability.

Long Answer Type Questions (Subjective)

1. Discuss the importance of solubility in the development and formulation of drugs, and explain how it can impact therapeutic effectiveness.

2. Describe the different methods for assessing drug solubility and their respective applications in pharmaceutical research.

3. Explain the role of pH in drug solubility, particularly focusing on weak acids and bases, and how this can be manipulated to improve drug delivery.

4. Discuss the impact of particle size on drug solubility and the techniques used to manipulate particle size in pharmaceutical formulations.

5. Explain the principles and applications of Henry's Law in the context of pharmaceutical sciences, particularly in the solubility of gases in liquids.

6. Describe the factors affecting drug solubility and how understanding these factors can aid in the optimization of drug formulations.

7. Discuss the concept of ideal and real solutions in the context of Raoult's Law, including the implications of deviations from ideal behavior in drug formulations.

8. Explain how the distribution law is used to optimize drug formulations and predict drug behavior in biological systems.

9. Discuss the applications and limitations of the distribution law in the context of drug solubility and pharmacokinetics.

10. Provide a detailed explanation of how solvation and association processes affect drug solubility and the formulation strategies used to enhance drug delivery and stability.

Answer Key

1. (C) Drug bioavailability
2. (A) Shake Flask Method
3. (D) Influences solubility especially for weak acids and bases
4. (A) Increases solubility
5. (C) Particle size of the drug
6. (C) Solubility of gases in liquids

7. (B) pH-dependent solubility

8. (D) Covalent bonding

9. (C) Smaller particles increase solubility

10. (C) It represents the maximum solubility of a compound

11. (C) Volume interaction parameter (δv)

12. (A) Entropy of mixing and interaction parameter

13. (A) The solubility of a solute between two non-miscible solvents

14. (B) Polar drugs

15. (C) Optimizing drug formulations

16. (C) Kinetic Solubility Studies

17. (C) Temperature at which two immiscible liquids become completely miscible

18. (B) Vapor pressure of the components

19. (A) The ratio of solubility of a drug in water to its solubility in oil

20. (B) Concentration of dissolved drug

CHAPTER – 2

STATES OF MATTER AND PROPERTIES OF MATTER

INTRODUCTION:

Introduction to States of Matter

Matter is anything that has mass and occupies space. It is composed of atoms and molecules, and it exists in different forms known as states of matter. The four fundamental states of matter are solid, liquid, gas, and plasma. Each state has distinct characteristics based on the arrangement and energy of its particles.

1. Solid

Characteristics:

a. **Definite Shape and Volume**: Solids maintain a fixed shape and volume.

b. **Particle Arrangement**: Particles are closely packed in a regular pattern.

c. **Particle Movement:** Particles vibrate around fixed positions but do not move freely.

d. **Incompressibility**: Solids are not easily compressible due to the tightly packed particles.

e. **Examples**: Ice, iron, diamond.

Properties:

a. **Density:** Generally higher than liquids and gases because of the close packing of particles.

b. **Rigidity:** Solids resist changes in shape and volume.

c. **Elasticity:** Ability to return to original shape after deformation.

d. **Thermal Expansion:** Solids expand slightly when heated due to increased vibration of particles.

2. Liquid

Characteristics:

a. **Definite Volume, Indefinite Shape**: Liquids take the shape of their container but have a fixed volume.

b. **Particle Arrangement**: Particles are close together but not in a fixed position, allowing them to flow.

c. **Particle Movement**: Particles move freely but stay in contact.

d. **Incompressibility:** Liquids are relatively incompressible.

e. **Examples:** Water, oil, alcohol.

Properties:

a. **Viscosity:** Resistance to flow; varies with temperature.

b. **Surface Tension**: The cohesive force at the surface of a liquid.

c. **Capillary Action**: The ability of a liquid to flow in narrow spaces against gravity.

d. **Diffusion**: Particles spread out over time from areas of high concentration to low concentration.

3. Gas

Characteristics:

a. **Indefinite Shape and Volume**: Gases take the shape and volume of their container.

b. **Particle Arrangement**: Particles are far apart with no regular arrangement.

c. **Particle Movement**: Particles move freely and rapidly in all directions.

d. **Compressibility**: Gases are highly compressible.

e. **Examples**: Oxygen, nitrogen, carbon dioxide.

Properties:

a. **Pressure**: The force that gas particles exert on the walls of their container.

b. **Temperature**: Directly related to the average kinetic energy of gas particles.

c. **Volume: Gases** expand to fill their container.

d. **Diffusion:** Gases mix evenly and completely when brought together.

e. **Boyle's Law**: Pressure is inversely proportional to volume at constant temperature.

f. **Charles's Law**: Volume is directly proportional to temperature at constant pressure.

4. Plasma

Characteristics:

a. **Indefinite Shape and Volume**: Like gases, plasmas take the shape and volume of their container.

b. **Particle Arrangement**: Consists of ionized particles - free electrons and ions.

c. **Particle Movement**: High-energy particles move freely.

d. **Conductivity**: Plasma conducts electricity and responds to magnetic fields.

e. **Examples:** Stars, neon signs, lightning.

Properties:

a. **Ionization:** Degree to which particles are ionized.

b. **Temperature**: Typically very high; necessary to maintain ionization.

c. **Magnetic Fields**: Can be confined and controlled using magnetic fields.

d. **Luminosity**: Often emits light due to the energy transitions of electrons.

Properties of Matter

1. Physical Properties:

a. **Mass and Weight**: Mass is the amount of matter, and weight is the force exerted by gravity on that mass.

b. **Volume**: The amount of space occupied by an object.

c. **Density**: Mass per unit volume.

d. **Melting and Boiling Points**: Temperatures at which matter changes state.

e. **Solubility**: Ability of a substance to dissolve in another substance.

f. **Conductivity**: Ability to conduct heat or electricity.

2. Chemical Properties:

a. **Reactivity**: Ability to undergo chemical changes.

b. **Flammability**: Ability to burn in the presence of oxygen.

c. **Oxidation States**: The charge of an atom in a compound.

d. **Acidity or Basicity**: pH level indicating acidic or basic nature.

e. **Toxicity:** Harmfulness to living organisms.

CHANGES IN THE STATE OF MATTER

Matter can transition between different states through physical processes that involve the addition or removal of energy. These changes are known as phase transitions and include processes such as melting, freezing, vaporization, condensation, sublimation, and deposition. Each process is associated with specific conditions of temperature and pressure.

1. Melting

Process:

a. Transition from solid to liquid.

b. Occurs when a solid absorbs heat, increasing the kinetic energy of its particles until they can overcome their fixed positions.

Key Points:

a. **Melting Point**: The temperature at which a solid becomes a liquid. For example, the melting point of ice is $0°C$ ($32°F$).

b. **Endothermic Process**: Requires the absorption of heat.

Example: Ice melting into water.

2. Freezing

Process:

a. Transition from liquid to solid.

b. Occurs when a liquid loses heat, decreasing the kinetic energy of its particles until they arrange into a fixed structure.

Key Points:

a. **Freezing Point**: The temperature at which a liquid becomes a solid. For water, it is 0°C (32°F).

b. **Exothermic Process**: Releases heat.

Example: Water freezing into ice.

3. Vaporization

Process:

a. Transition from liquid to gas.

b. Can occur through evaporation or boiling.

Key Points:

a. **Evaporation:** Occurs at the surface of a liquid at temperatures below the boiling point.

b. **Boiling**: Occurs throughout the liquid at the boiling point.

c. **Boiling Point**: The temperature at which a liquid becomes a gas. For water, it is 100°C (212°F) at standard atmospheric pressure.

d. Endothermic Process: Requires the absorption of heat.

Example: Water boiling into steam.

4. Condensation

Process:

a. Transition from gas to liquid.

b. Occurs when a gas loses heat, reducing the kinetic energy of its particles, allowing them to come closer together to form a liquid.

Key Points:

a. **Dew Point**: The temperature at which condensation occurs.

b. **Exothermic Process**: Releases heat.

Example: Steam condensing into water droplets.

5. Sublimation

Process:

a. Transition from solid to gas without passing through the liquid state.

b. Occurs when a solid absorbs heat enough to directly convert into a gas.

Key Points:

Endothermic Process: Requires the absorption of heat.

Example: Dry ice (solid carbon dioxide) sublimating into carbon dioxide gas.

6. Deposition

Process:

a. Transition from gas to solid without passing through the liquid state.

b. Occurs when a gas loses enough heat to directly convert into a solid.

Key Points:

Exothermic Process: Releases heat.

Example: Frost forming on a cold surface from water vapor in the air.

Properties of Matter

Matter can be described through its physical and chemical properties, which determine how it behaves under various conditions.

Physical Properties:

a. **Mass and Weight**: Mass is the measure of the amount of matter in an object, while weight is the gravitational force acting on that mass.

b. **Volume**: The amount of space occupied by an object.

c. **Density**: Mass per unit volume, often measured in grams per cubic centimeter (g/cm^3).

d. **Melting and Boiling Points**: Temperatures at which a substance changes state.

e. **Solubility:** The ability of a substance to dissolve in another substance.

f. **Conductivity:** Ability to conduct heat or electricity.

g. **Malleability:** Ability to be hammered or rolled into thin sheets.

h. **Ductility:** Ability to be drawn into wires.

Chemical Properties:

a. **Reactivity**: How readily a substance undergoes chemical changes.

b. **Flammability**: Ability to burn in the presence of oxygen.

c. **Oxidation States**: The degree of oxidation of an atom in a compound.

d. **Acidity or Basicity**: Measured by pH, indicating how acidic or basic a substance is.

e. **Toxicity:** The degree to which a substance can harm living organisms.

LATENT HEATS

Latent heat refers to the amount of heat energy required to change the state of a substance without changing its temperature. During phase transitions, such as melting, freezing, vaporization, condensation, sublimation, and deposition, energy is either absorbed or released by the substance. This energy is used to overcome the intermolecular forces holding the particles together in one phase, enabling the transition to another phase. There are two main types of latent heat: latent heat of fusion and latent heat of vaporization.

1. Latent Heat of Fusion

Definition:

The amount of heat energy required to change 1 kilogram of a substance from a solid to a liquid (or vice versa) at its melting point, without changing its temperature.

Key Points:

a. **Melting (Solid to Liquid)**: Absorbs heat.

b. **Freezing (Liquid to Solid)**: Releases heat.

c. **Units**: Typically measured in joules per kilogram (J/kg).

Example:

a. For water, the latent heat of fusion is approximately 334,000 J/kg. This means 334,000 joules of energy are required to melt 1 kilogram of ice at 0°C without changing its temperature.

2. Latent Heat of Vaporization

Definition:

The amount of heat energy required to change 1 kilogram of a substance from a liquid to a gas (or vice versa) at its boiling point, without changing its temperature.

Key Points:

1. **Vaporization (Liquid to Gas):** Absorbs heat.
2. **Condensation (Gas to Liquid):** Releases heat.
3. **Units:** Typically measured in joules per kilogram (J/kg).

Example:

For water, the latent heat of vaporization is approximately 2,260,000 J/kg. This means 2,260,000 joules of energy are required to convert 1 kilogram of water to steam at 100°C without changing its temperature.

Other Phase Changes:

Latent Heat of Sublimation: The amount of heat required to change 1 kilogram of a substance from a solid to a gas (or vice versa) without passing through the liquid phase. **Example:** For carbon dioxide (dry ice), sublimation occurs at -78.5°C, and the latent heat of sublimation is about 571,000 J/kg.

Understanding Latent Heat in the Context of State Changes

Melting and Freezing:

1. When a solid melts, it absorbs heat energy (latent heat of fusion) to break the bonds holding the particles in a fixed structure.
2. When a liquid freezes, it releases the same amount of heat energy to form those bonds and create a solid structure.

Vaporization and Condensation:

1. During vaporization, a liquid absorbs heat energy (latent heat of vaporization) to allow particles to escape into the gas phase.
2. During condensation, a gas releases the same amount of heat energy to form bonds and transition into the liquid phase.

Sublimation and Deposition:

1. During sublimation, a solid absorbs heat energy to transition directly into the gas phase.
2. During deposition, a gas releases heat energy to transition directly into the solid phase.

Importance of Latent Heat

1. Weather and Climate:

1. **Evaporation and Condensation**: The latent heat of vaporization and condensation plays a crucial role in the water cycle, affecting weather patterns and climate.
2. **Storm Formation**: The release of latent heat during condensation fuels storms and hurricanes, providing the energy needed for their development.

2. Industrial Applications:

1. **Refrigeration and Air Conditioning**: Utilizes the principles of latent heat during the evaporation and condensation of refrigerants to transfer heat and provide cooling.
2. **Heat Engines**: Steam engines and other heat engines rely on the latent heat of vaporization of water to convert thermal energy into mechanical work.

3. Everyday Phenomena:

1. **Sweating**: When we sweat, our body uses the latent heat of vaporization to cool down as the sweat evaporates from our skin.
2. **Cooking:** The latent heat of fusion and vaporization are involved in processes like melting butter or boiling water, which are common in cooking.

Properties of Matter Related to Latent Heat

Physical Properties:

1. **Thermal Conductivity**: Affects the rate at which heat is absorbed or released during phase transitions.

2. **Specific Heat Capacity**: The amount of heat required to change the temperature of a substance, important for understanding how substances react to heat before reaching the latent heat stage.

Chemical Properties:

1. **Intermolecular Force**s: Stronger intermolecular forces require more latent heat to overcome, affecting melting and boiling points.

2. **Chemical Stability:** Substances with high latent heats often have stable structures that require significant energy to change state.

VAPOUR PRESSURE

Vapour pressure is the pressure exerted by the vapour (gas phase) of a substance in equilibrium with its liquid or solid phase at a given temperature. It is a key concept in understanding the behavior of substances in different states of matter and their transitions between these states.

Definition and Explanation

Vapour Pressure:

1. The pressure exerted by a vapour in thermodynamic equilibrium with its condensed phases (liquid or solid) in a closed system.

2. It indicates the tendency of particles to escape from the liquid or solid phase into the gas phase.

Equilibrium:

1. When a liquid is placed in a closed container, molecules evaporate and enter the gas phase.

2. Some of these gas molecules will collide with the liquid surface and condense back into the liquid.

3. Equilibrium is reached when the rate of evaporation equals the rate of condensation, resulting in a constant vapour pressure.

Factors Affecting Vapour Pressure

1. **Temperature:**

   a. Vapour pressure increases with temperature because higher temperatures provide more energy to molecules, allowing more to escape into the gas phase.

   b. **Clausius-Clapeyron Equation**: Describes the relationship between vapour pressure and temperature.

   $$\ln⁡ P = -\Delta Hva(1T) + C$$

where

   a. P is the vapour pressure,

   b. $\Delta Hvap$ is the enthalpy of vaporization,

   c. R is the gas constant,

   d. T is the temperature, and

   e. C is a constant.

2. **Nature of the Liquid:**

   a. Liquids with weaker intermolecular forces (e.g., van der Waals forces) have higher vapour pressures because molecules can escape more easily.

   b. Liquids with stronger intermolecular forces (e.g., hydrogen bonds) have lower vapour pressures.

Measuring Vapour Pressure

Dynamic Method:

A liquid is placed in a closed container, and the pressure is measured as the system reaches equilibrium.

Static Method:

The pressure in the closed container is measured directly after equilibrium has been established.

Vapour Pressure and Boiling Point

Boiling Point:

1. The temperature at which the vapour pressure of a liquid equals the external pressure (usually atmospheric pressure).

2. Normal Boiling Point: The boiling point of a liquid at 1 atmosphere (101.3 kPa) of pressure.

Relationship:

1. A liquid boil when its vapour pressure equals the surrounding atmospheric pressure.

2. At higher altitudes, atmospheric pressure is lower, so liquids boil at lower temperatures.

Vapour Pressure in Different States of Matter

1. Solids

Sublimation:

1. Some solids, like dry ice (solid CO_2), have a significant vapour pressure and can sublime directly from the solid to the gas phase.

2. The vapour pressure of solids is usually much lower than that of liquids at the same temperature.

2. Liquids

Volatile Liquids:

1. Liquids with high vapour pressures at a given temperature are considered volatile (e.g., ethanol, acetone).

2. Non-volatile liquids have low vapour pressures (e.g., water, glycerol).

3. Gases

Condensation:

1. Gases will condense into the liquid phase when the vapour pressure exceeds the pressure of the gas phase in the environment.

2. Dew point: The temperature at which air becomes saturated with water vapour and condensation begins.

Applications and Importance of Vapour Pressure

1. Weather and Climate:

a. Vapour pressure is crucial in meteorology for predicting condensation, cloud formation, and precipitation.

b. High humidity indicates high vapour pressure of water in the air.

2. Chemical Engineering:

a. Designing distillation processes relies on differences in vapour pressure between components to separate mixtures.

b. Understanding vapour pressure is essential in designing storage containers for volatile liquids to prevent evaporation losses.

3. Pharmaceuticals:

Vapour pressure data helps in formulating and storing drugs to ensure stability and efficacy.

4. Food Industry:

a. Used in processes like freeze-drying, which relies on sublimation under reduced pressure to preserve food.

Properties of Matter Related to Vapour Pressure

Physical Properties:

1. **Volatility**: The tendency of a substance to vaporize; directly related to vapour pressure.

2. **Boiling Point:** Dependent on vapour pressure; substances with high vapour pressures boil at lower temperatures.

3. **Intermolecular Forces**: Stronger forces result in lower vapour pressures and higher boiling points.

Chemical Properties:

1. **Chemical Stability**: Substances with low vapour pressures are often more chemically stable at given temperatures.

2. **Reactivity:** Volatile substances with high vapour pressures may be more reactive due to increased availability of molecules in the gas phase.

SUBLIMATION CRITICAL POINT

Sublimation and the critical point are essential concepts in understanding the phase transitions and behavior of matter. Here, we explore these phenomena in detail, including their definitions, characteristics, and implications in various contexts.

Sublimation

Definition:

Sublimation is the phase transition in which a substance changes directly from a solid to a gas without passing through the liquid phase. This process occurs under specific conditions of temperature and pressure.

Key Points:

1. **Endothermic Process**: Requires the absorption of heat energy.
2. **Conditions**: Typically occurs at low pressures and/or low temperatures where the liquid phase is not stable.

Examples:

1. **Dry Ice (Solid CO2):** Sublimates at -78.5°C at standard atmospheric pressure.
2. **Iodine**: Sublimates directly to violet gas upon heating.
3. **Snow and Ice**: Can sublimate in cold, dry conditions, bypassing the liquid phase.

Applications:

1. **Freeze-Drying (Lyophilization):** Used in pharmaceuticals and food preservation to remove water from perishable materials.
2. **Purification:** Sublimation can purify compounds, such as in the purification of naphthalene.

The Sublimation Curve and Phase Diagram

Sublimation Curve:

A plot on a phase diagram that shows the conditions of temperature and pressure at which sublimation occurs. It separates the solid and gas regions on the phase diagram.

Phase Diagram:

1. A graphical representation of the physical states of a substance under different conditions of temperature and pressure.
2. **Triple Point**: The unique set of conditions where all three phases (solid, liquid, and gas) coexist in equilibrium.
3. **Sublimation Curve:** Extends from the triple point to the point where the solid and gas phases exist in equilibrium.

Critical Point

Definition:

The critical point is the end point of the phase equilibrium curve between the liquid and gas phases. At this point, the properties of the liquid and gas phases become indistinguishable, leading to a single phase known as a supercritical fluid.

Key Points:

1. **Critical Temperature (T_c)**: The temperature above which a substance cannot exist as a liquid, regardless of pressure.
2. **Critical Pressure (P_c):** The pressure required to liquefy a substance at its critical temperature.
3. **Supercritical Fluid:** A state of matter beyond the critical point where the substance exhibits properties of both liquids and gases.

Example:

Water: Critical temperature is 374°C, and critical pressure is 22.1 MPa.

Applications:

1. **Supercritical Fluid Extraction**: Used in the decaffeination of coffee and extraction of essential oils.
2. **Chemical Reactions**: Supercritical fluids can act as solvents with unique properties, enhancing reaction rates and selectivity.

Understanding the Critical Point on a Phase Diagram

Phase Diagram Features:

1. **Triple Point:** Indicates the conditions where solid, liquid, and gas phases coexist.

2. **Critical Point:** Marks the end of the liquid-gas equilibrium curve.

3. **Supercritical Region**: Area beyond the critical point where the substance exists as a supercritical fluid.

Behavior at the Critical Point:

1. **Density**: The densities of the liquid and gas phases become equal.

2. **Surface Tension**: Approaches zero as the distinction between liquid and gas phases disappears.

3. **Unique Properties**: Supercritical fluids can diffuse through solids like gases and dissolve materials like liquids.

Properties of Matter Related to Sublimation and Critical Point

Physical Properties:

1. **Phase Transition Temperatures**: Melting, boiling, and sublimation points are crucial for determining the conditions for phase changes.

2. **Density and Compressibility**: Change significantly near the critical point, affecting material properties and applications.

Chemical Properties:

1. **Reactivity:** Supercritical fluids can enhance chemical reactions due to their unique solvating properties.

2. **Solubility:** Solubility of substances in supercritical fluids can be tuned by adjusting temperature and pressure.

EUTECTIC MIXTURES

Eutectic mixtures are an important concept in the study of materials science and phase transitions. They are mixtures of two or more components that solidify at a lower temperature than any of the individual components, forming a unique microstructure and exhibiting distinct physical properties.

Eutectic Mixture:

1. A eutectic mixture is a homogeneous mixture of substances that melts or solidifies at a single temperature, which is lower than the melting points of the individual components.
2. The eutectic point is the specific composition and temperature at which the eutectic mixture transitions between solid and liquid phases.

Eutectic Point:

1. **Temperature**: The lowest possible melting point of the mixture.
2. **Composition**: The specific ratio of components that forms the eutectic mixture.

Phase Diagram of Eutectic Systems

A phase diagram for a eutectic system typically includes:

1. **Liquidus Line**: Above which the mixture is entirely liquid.
2. **Solidus Line:** Below which the mixture is entirely solid.
3. **Eutectic Point**: Where the liquidus and solidus lines meet, indicating the composition and temperature at which the eutectic mixture melts or solidifies.

Example:

Lead-Tin Alloy: A common eutectic system with a eutectic point at approximately 183°C and 61.9% tin by weight.

Formation of Eutectic Mixtures

Solidification Process:

1. **Cooling**: As the liquid mixture cools down, it reaches the eutectic temperature.
2. **Simultaneous Crystallization**: Both components crystallize simultaneously from the liquid mixture at the eutectic composition, forming a fine, interlocking microstructure of the two solid phases.

Properties of Eutectic Mixtures

1. Lower Melting Point:

Eutectic mixtures melt at a lower temperature than any of the pure components, making them useful in applications requiring precise melting points.

2. Homogeneous Microstructure:

The eutectic mixture solidifies into a fine, homogeneous microstructure, providing unique mechanical properties.

3. Enhanced Properties:

Eutectic alloys often have enhanced mechanical properties, such as increased hardness or better wear resistance, compared to their individual components.

Applications of Eutectic Mixtures

1. Soldering:

Eutectic solders, such as lead-tin solder, are widely used in electronics because of their low melting point and reliable bonding properties.

2. Metal Casting:

Eutectic alloys are used in metal casting to achieve precise melting and solidification behaviors, improving the quality and performance of cast components.

3. Phase Change Materials:

Eutectic mixtures are used as phase change materials (PCMs) for thermal energy storage, leveraging their ability to absorb and release large amounts of latent heat at a specific temperature.

4. Cryogenics:

Eutectic mixtures can be used in cryogenic applications to maintain low temperatures for biological and industrial processes.

Eutectic Systems in Nature and Industry

Natural Occurrences:

Salt-Water Systems: Natural eutectic mixtures of salts in seawater can form brine at lower freezing points, influencing oceanic and polar processes.

Industrial Alloys:

Aluminum-Silicon Alloys: Used in automotive and aerospace industries for their lightweight and high-strength properties.

Food Industry:

Eutectic Freezing: Utilized in freeze-drying processes to lower the freezing point of food mixtures, preserving quality and extending shelf life.

Properties of Matter Related to Eutectic Mixtures

Physical Properties:

1. **Thermal Conductivity**: Eutectic mixtures often have higher thermal conductivities, useful in applications requiring efficient heat transfer.
2. **Density and Viscosity**: Eutectic compositions can influence the density and viscosity of the mixture, impacting flow and processing characteristics.

Chemical Properties:

1. **Chemical Stability**: The stability of eutectic mixtures can vary depending on the components, influencing their reactivity and compatibility with other materials.
2. **Corrosion Resistance**: Eutectic alloys can exhibit improved corrosion resistance, important for durability in various environments.

Gases

Gases are one of the fundamental states of matter, characterized by their ability to expand and fill any container, low density, and high compressibility. Understanding the properties and behavior of gases is crucial in fields such as chemistry, physics, engineering, and environmental science.

Characteristics of Gases

1. **Expansion:**
    a. Gases expand to fill the shape and volume of their containers due to the high kinetic energy of their molecules.

2. **Low Density:**
    a. Gases have much lower densities compared to solids and liquids because their molecules are far apart.

3. **Compressibility:**
    a. Gases can be easily compressed since the space between molecules allows them to be pushed closer together.

4. **Diffuse Rapidly:**
    a. Gas molecules move rapidly and spread out quickly to uniformly distribute themselves within a container.

Properties of Gases

1. Volume (V):

The amount of space that a gas occupies, typically measured in liters (L) or cubic meters (m^3).

2. Pressure (P):

The force exerted by gas molecules colliding with the walls of their container, measured in atmospheres (atm), pascals (Pa), or millimeters of mercury (mmHg).

3. Temperature (T):

A measure of the average kinetic energy of gas molecules, typically measured in Kelvin (K).

4. Number of Moles (n):

The amount of substance, measured in moles (mol), which correlates to the number of molecules present in the gas.

Gas Laws

Gas behavior is described by several fundamental laws that relate volume, pressure, temperature, and number of moles:

1. Boyle's Law:

$$P \propto 1 \text{(at constant T and n)}$$

Pressure inversely proportional to volume when temperature and number of moles are constant.

$$P1V1 = P2V2$$

2. Charles's Law:

$$V \propto \text{(at constant P and n)}$$

$$V \propto T \text{(at constant P and n)}$$

1. Volume directly proportional to temperature when pressure and number of moles are constant.

$$V1T1 = V2T2$$

3. Avogadro's Law:

$$V \propto \text{(at constant P and T)}$$

$$V \propto n \text{(at constant P and T)}$$

1. Volume directly proportional to the number of moles when pressure and temperature are constant.
2. $V1n1 = V2n2$

4. Ideal Gas Law:

$$PV = nRT$$

$$PV = nRT$$

1. Combines Boyle's, Charles's, and Avogadro's laws into one equation, where
2. R is the universal gas constant (8.314 J/(mol\cdotpK)

5. Dalton's Law of Partial Pressures:

$$P\text{total} = P1 + P2 + P3 + \cdots$$

The total pressure exerted by a mixture of gases is the sum of the partial pressures of each individual gas.

Kinetic Molecular Theory

The kinetic molecular theory explains the behavior of gases based on the idea that gas molecules are in constant, random motion:

1. Gas molecules are in continuous, random motion.
2. The volume of individual gas molecules is negligible compared to the volume of the container.
3. Intermolecular forces between gas molecules are negligible.
4. Collisions between gas molecules and with the walls of the container are perfectly elastic.
5. The average kinetic energy of gas molecules is proportional to the temperature in Kelvin.

Real Gases vs. Ideal Gases

Ideal Gases:

1. Follow the ideal gas law precisely.
2. No intermolecular forces and occupy no volume.

Real Gases:

1. Deviate from ideal behavior under high pressure and low temperature due to intermolecular forces and finite molecular volume.
2. Described by the Van der Waals equation:

$$(P + aV2)(V - b) = nRT$$

where

a and b are constants specific to each gas, accounting for intermolecular forces and molecular volume, respectively.

Applications of Gases

1. Industrial Processes:

a. **Gas Production**: Oxygen, nitrogen, and argon production via air separation plants.

b. **Chemical Synthesis**: Ammonia synthesis in the Haber process using nitrogen and hydrogen gases.

2. Medical Uses:

a. **Respiratory Therapies**: Oxygen therapy for patients with breathing difficulties.

b. **Anesthesia:** Use of gases like nitrous oxide and halothane.

3. Environmental Science:

a. **Greenhouse Gases**: Understanding the impact of gases like CO2 and methane on climate change.

b. **Air Quality Monitoring**: Measuring pollutant gases to assess and improve air quality.

4. Everyday Life:

a. **Cooking:** Use of propane or natural gas for heating and cooking.

b. **Inflation:** Helium for balloons and air for tires.

AEROSOLS– INHALERS

Aerosols and inhalers are practical applications of the principles of matter, particularly focusing on the gaseous state and particle suspensions. They are crucial in various fields, including healthcare, environmental science, and industry. This section explores the science behind aerosols and inhalers, their properties, and their applications.

Aerosols

Definition:

Aerosols are suspensions of fine solid particles or liquid droplets in a gas. They can be natural (like mist and volcanic ash) or anthropogenic (like spray paints and medical inhalers).

Characteristics of Aerosols:

1. **Particle Size**: Ranges from a few nanometers to several micrometers.

2. **Dispersion Medium**: The gas in which particles are suspended, typically air.

3. **Stability**: Depends on particle size, density, and interactions between particles and the dispersion medium.

Properties of Aerosols

1. **Size and Distribution:**

    a. Particle size affects the behavior, stability, and distribution of aerosols.

    b. Fine particles (below 2.5 micrometers) can remain suspended longer and penetrate deeper into the respiratory system.

2. **Surface Area:**

    a. High surface area to volume ratio, which influences reactivity and interaction with the environment.

3. **Optical Properties:**

    a. Aerosols scatter and absorb light, impacting visibility and climate.

4. **Chemical Composition:**

    a. Can vary widely, including organic compounds, salts, metals, and biological materials.

Applications of Aerosols

1. **Medical Inhalers:**

    a. Deliver medication directly to the lungs for respiratory conditions like asthma and COPD.

2. **Environmental Monitoring:**

    a. Study of air quality and the impact of pollutants on health and climate.

3. **Industrial Uses:**

    a. Spray paints, coatings, and pesticides.

4. **Consumer Products:**

    a. Aerosol cans for deodorants, insecticides, and cleaning agents.

Inhalers

Inhalers are medical devices designed to deliver medication to the lungs in the form of aerosols. They are commonly used to treat respiratory conditions such as asthma, chronic obstructive pulmonary disease (COPD), and other lung diseases.

Types of Inhalers:

1. **Metered-Dose Inhalers (MDIs):**
    a. Deliver a specific amount of medication in aerosol form using a propellant.
    b. Components include a canister, actuator, and metering valve.

2. **Dry Powder Inhalers (DPIs):**
    a. Deliver medication in powder form without the need for a propellant.
    b. Activated by the patient's breath, which disperses the powder into the lungs.

3. **Nebulizers:**
    a. Convert liquid medication into a fine mist for inhalation.
    b. Used for patients who have difficulty using MDIs or DPIs.

Mechanism of Inhalers

1. **Aerosol Generation:**
    a. MDIs use propellants to create aerosolized medication.
    b. DPIs rely on the patient's inhalation to disperse the powder.
    c. Nebulizers use a compressor to generate a mist from liquid medication.

2. **Particle Size:**
    a. Optimal particle size for deep lung penetration is between 1 to 5 micrometers.
    b. Smaller particles can reach the alveoli, while larger particles deposit in the upper airways.

3. Deposition and Absorption:

    a. Medication must deposit in the respiratory tract to be effective.

    b. Factors affecting deposition include particle size, inhalation technique, and lung function.

Advantages of Inhalers

1. Direct Delivery:

    a. Medication is delivered directly to the lungs, leading to rapid onset of action.

    b. Reduces systemic side effects compared to oral medications.

2. Portability:

    a. MDIs and DPIs are compact and portable, allowing for easy use and convenience.

3. Controlled Dosage:

    a. MDIs provide precise dosing with each actuation.

Challenges and Considerations

1. Inhalation Technique:

    a. Proper technique is crucial for effective delivery.

    b. Patients must be trained on how to use their inhalers correctly.

2. Environmental Impact:

    a. Propellants in MDIs, such as hydrofluoroalkanes (HFAs), have less environmental impact than older chlorofluorocarbons (CFCs) but still contribute to greenhouse gases.

3. Medication Stability:

    a. Formulations must remain stable in aerosol form for effective treatment.

Properties of Matter Related to Aerosols and Inhalers

1. Physical Properties:

    a. **Viscosity and Surface Tension**: Affect the formation and stability of aerosols.

b. **Density and Buoyancy**: Influence the suspension and deposition of particles.

2. **Chemical Properties:**

    a. **Reactivity**: Aerosol particles can undergo chemical reactions in the atmosphere or in the respiratory system.

    b. **Solubility:** Determines how medication is absorbed and distributed in the lungs.

RELATIVE HUMIDITY

Relative humidity is an important concept in understanding the interaction between the gaseous state of matter (specifically water vapor) and its effects on various physical and chemical properties of the environment. This section explores relative humidity in detail, including its definition, measurement, significance, and impact on different phenomena.

Relative Humidity (RH):

Definition: Relative humidity is the ratio of the current amount of water vapor in the air to the maximum amount of water vapor the air can hold at a specific temperature, expressed as a percentage.

RH=(Actual Vapor PressureSaturation Vapor Pressure)×100%

Saturation Vapor Pressure:

The maximum pressure exerted by water vapor in the air at a given temperature. It increases with temperature.

Measurement of Relative Humidity

Hygrometers:

Instruments used to measure relative humidity. There are several types, including mechanical hygrometers, electronic hygrometers, and psychrometers.

Psychrometer:

Consists of two thermometers, one with a wet bulb and one with a dry bulb. The difference in readings between the two thermometers is used to calculate relative humidity using psychrometric charts or equations.

Electronic Hygrometers:

Use sensors to measure changes in electrical resistance or capacitance caused by humidity.

Importance of Relative Humidity

1. **Human Comfort:**

    a. Relative humidity affects thermal comfort. Ideal indoor humidity levels are typically between 30% and 50%.

2. **Health:**

    a. High RH can promote the growth of mold, dust mites, and bacteria, affecting respiratory health.

    b. Low RH can cause dry skin, irritation, and respiratory discomfort.

3. **Weather and Climate:**

    a. Relative humidity is a key factor in weather forecasting and understanding climate patterns.

    b. High RH can lead to the formation of dew, fog, and precipitation.

4. **Industrial Applications:**

    a. Critical in processes like drying, fermentation, and chemical manufacturing.

    b. Ensures the quality and stability of products in industries like pharmaceuticals, food, and electronics.

5. **Agriculture:**

    a. Affects plant transpiration, soil moisture, and the occurrence of plant diseases.

Properties of Matter Related to Relative Humidity

1. Evaporation and Condensation:

RH influences the rate of evaporation and condensation of water. High RH slows down evaporation while promoting condensation.

2. Dew Point:

The temperature at which air becomes saturated with moisture and water vapor begins to condense into liquid. A higher RH means the dew point is closer to the current air temperature.

3. Hygroscopic Materials:

Substances that absorb moisture from the air. RH affects their behavior, as seen in materials like wood, paper, and certain chemicals.

Psychrometric Chart

A psychrometric chart graphically represents the physical and thermal properties of moist air. Key parameters include:

1. **Dry-Bulb Temperature**: The air temperature measured by a regular thermometer.
2. **Wet-Bulb Temperature**: The temperature measured by a thermometer covered in a water-soaked cloth, accounting for cooling by evaporation.
3. **Dew Point**: The temperature at which air reaches saturation and water vapor condenses.
4. **Humidity Ratio**: The amount of water vapor per unit mass of dry air.
5. **Enthalpy**: The total heat content of the air-water vapor mixture.

Applications of Relative Humidity

1. HVAC Systems:

    a. Heating, ventilation, and air conditioning systems use RH to maintain comfortable indoor environments.

2. Meteorology:

    a. Weather prediction models incorporate RH to forecast precipitation, fog, and storms.

3. Museums and Archives:

a. RH control is crucial to preserving artifacts, manuscripts, and artworks.

4. Building Construction:

a. Understanding RH helps in designing buildings for better moisture control and energy efficiency.

Effects of Relative Humidity on Materials

1. Metals:

High RH can accelerate corrosion in metals through the formation of a thin water layer that facilitates electrochemical reactions.

2. Polymers:

RH can affect the mechanical properties and dimensional stability of polymers, leading to swelling or shrinking.

3. Foods:

RH impacts the shelf life and quality of food products. High RH can cause spoilage and mold growth, while low RH can lead to drying and texture changes.

4. Electronics:

RH control is essential to prevent condensation and corrosion in sensitive electronic components.

LIQUID COMPLEXES

The concept of "liquid complexes" isn't commonly used in the context of states of matter or properties of matter. However, I can provide information about liquid complexes in the context of coordination chemistry, where the term is occasionally used.

Liquid Complexes in Coordination Chemistry

In coordination chemistry, liquid complexes refer to solutions containing coordination compounds or complexes dissolved in a liquid solvent. Coordination compounds are molecules or ions composed of a central metal atom or ion bonded to surrounding ligands through coordinate covalent bonds.

Properties of Liquid Complexes

1. **Solubility:**

   a. Liquid complexes are typically soluble in the solvent, forming stable solutions. The solubility depends on the nature of the coordination compound and the solvent used.

2. **Stability:**

   a. Liquid complexes can exhibit varying degrees of stability depending on factors such as ligand strength, metal-ligand bonding, and solvent-solute interactions.

3. **Conductivity:**

   a. Some liquid complexes may exhibit conductivity due to the presence of ions in solution, especially if the coordination compound dissociates into ions.

4. **Color:**

   a. Many coordination compounds are colored due to the presence of transition metal ions. The color of the liquid complex solution can vary depending on the metal ion and ligands involved.

5. **Reactivity:**

   a. Liquid complexes can participate in chemical reactions, including ligand exchange reactions, redox reactions, and coordination isomerism.

6. **Viscosity and Density:**

   a. The viscosity and density of liquid complexes solutions depend on the solvent used and the concentration of the coordination compound.

Applications of Liquid Complexes

1. **Analytical Chemistry:**

a. Liquid complexes are used in analytical techniques such as spectrophotometry and chromatography for the detection and analysis of metal ions.

2. **Catalysis:**

   a. Some liquid complexes serve as catalysts in various chemical reactions, including industrial processes and organic synthesis.

3. **Biological Systems:**

   a. Liquid complexes have applications in bioinorganic chemistry and biochemistry, where they can interact with biological molecules and systems.

4. **Material Science:**

   a. Liquid complexes play a role in the synthesis of materials with specific properties, such as nanoparticles, thin films, and coordination polymers.

Factors Affecting Liquid Complexes

1. **Nature of the Metal Ion:**

   a. The choice of metal ion influences the properties and reactivity of the liquid complex.

2. **Nature of Ligands:**

   a. Different ligands can form complexes with the metal ion, affecting the stability, color, and other properties of the liquid complex.

3. **Solvent Effects:**

   a. The solvent used can influence the solubility, stability, and other properties of the liquid complex.

4. **pH and Ionic Strength:**

   a. pH and ionic strength can affect the speciation and stability of the liquid complex in solution.

LIQUID CRYSTALS

Liquid crystals are a fascinating state of matter that exhibit properties of both liquids and crystalline solids. They have unique structural and optical properties, making them useful in a wide range of applications, from electronic displays to biological systems. Let's delve into the details of liquid crystals, their properties, and their significance.

Definition:

Liquid crystals are a state of matter that lies between the solid and liquid states. They possess long-range order in one or two dimensions like a solid but retain the mobility of molecules characteristic of liquids.

Characteristics:

1. **Anisotropy**: Liquid crystals have different properties along different axes due to their ordered structure.
2. **Flow Properties**: They flow like liquids but maintain a degree of molecular alignment.
3. **Response to External Stimuli**: Liquid crystals can respond to changes in temperature, pressure, electric fields, and mechanical stress.

Types of Liquid Crystals

1. **Nematic Liquid Crystals:**
   a. Molecules align along a single direction, giving them a long-range orientational order but no positional order.
2. **Smectic liquid crystals:**
   a. Molecules arrange themselves in layers, with each layer exhibiting long-range order, but the molecules within each layer can move freely.
3. **Cholesteric (chiral nematic) liquid crystals:**
   a. Similar to nematic liquid crystals but with a twist in the molecular alignment, leading to a helical structure.
4. **Columnar (hexatic) liquid crystals:**
   a. Molecules arrange themselves in columns, exhibiting long-range order in two dimensions.

Properties of liquid crystals

1. **Optical properties:**

   a. Liquid crystals are optically anisotropic, meaning their optical properties vary with direction.

   b. They exhibit birefringence, meaning they have different refractive indices along different axes.

   c. Changes in molecular orientation can lead to changes in optical properties, such as polarization and color.

2. **Thermal properties:**

   a. Liquid crystals have distinct phase transition temperatures, including melting points and clearing points.

   b. They may exhibit thermotropic behavior, where phase transitions occur in response to changes in temperature.

3. **Electrical Properties:**

   a. Liquid crystals can respond to electric fields, leading to changes in molecular orientation.

   b. This property is exploited in liquid crystal displays (LCDs) for electronic devices.

4. **Viscoelastic properties:**

   a. Liquid crystals exhibit both viscous and elastic behavior, allowing them to deform and flow under stress while retaining some degree of shape memory.

Applications of liquid crystals

1. **Liquid crystal displays (lcds):**

   a. LCDs are the most well-known application of liquid crystals, used in televisions, computer monitors, smartphones, and other electronic devices.

2. **Optical devices:**

a. Liquid crystals are used in optical filters, polarizers, and variable optical attenuators.

3. **Biomedical applications:**

    a. Liquid crystals have applications in biosensing, drug delivery systems, and the study of biomembranes.

4. **Photonics and nanotechnology:**

    a. Liquid crystals are used in photonic crystals, photonic bandgap fibers, and metamaterials for controlling light propagation.

5. **Chemical and materials science:**

    a. Liquid crystals are valuable tools for studying molecular self-assembly, phase transitions, and soft matter physics.

LIQUID CRYSTALS IN NATURE

1. **Biological systems:**

    a. Liquid crystalline phases are found in biological systems, such as cell membranes, DNA, and certain protein structures.

    b. They play essential roles in biological functions, including cell signaling and organization.

2. **Bioinspired materials:**

    a. Researchers draw inspiration from natural liquid crystals to design biomimetic materials with tunable properties for various applications.

GLASSY STATES

The glassy state is a distinct phase of matter with properties that lie between those of crystalline solids and liquids. This state arises from the rapid cooling of a liquid below its melting point, resulting in the absence of a regular crystalline structure. Glassy materials exhibit unique physical, mechanical, and thermal properties that make them essential in various applications. Let's explore glassy states in detail, including their properties and significance.

Definition:

The glassy state is a non-crystalline, amorphous phase of matter formed by the solidification of a liquid without the formation of a regular crystalline structure.

Characteristics:

1. **Amorphous Structure**: Glassy materials lack the long-range order characteristic of crystalline solids.

2. **Rigidity**: They are typically rigid and brittle due to the lack of structural regularity.

3. **Transparency:** Many glassy materials are transparent or translucent, allowing light to pass through.

4. **High Viscosity**: Although solid, glassy materials have viscosities that are orders of magnitude higher than those of crystalline solids.

Formation of Glassy States

The formation of a glassy state involves the rapid cooling of a liquid, preventing the orderly arrangement of atoms or molecules that typically occurs during crystallization. This rapid cooling inhibits the formation of crystalline nuclei, leading to the formation of an amorphous, glassy structure.

Types of Glassy Materials

1. **Silicate Glasses:**

   a. Most common type, composed primarily of silicon dioxide (SiO_2) and other metal oxides.

   b. Include soda-lime glass, borosilicate glass, and fused quartz.

2. **Polymeric Glasses:**

   a. Formed from organic polymers, such as polystyrene, poly(methyl methacrylate) (PMMA), and polyethylene terephthalate (PET).

3. **Metallic Glasses (Amorphous Metals):**

   a. Alloys with disordered atomic arrangements, typically formed by rapid solidification techniques.

4. **Composite Glasses:**

   a. Glasses formed from a combination of different materials, such as glass-ceramics.

Properties of Glassy States

1. **Mechanical Properties:**

   a. Glassy materials are generally hard, brittle, and have low tensile strength.

   b. They lack the plasticity and ductility observed in crystalline solids.

2. **Thermal Properties:**

   a. Glassy materials have relatively low thermal conductivity.

   b. They exhibit thermal expansion behavior distinct from that of crystalline solids.

3. **Optical Properties:**

   a. Many glassy materials are transparent or translucent, with optical properties that can be tailored for specific applications.

   b. Some glasses exhibit optical effects such as birefringence or fluorescence.

4. **Chemical Stability:**

   a. Glassy materials are often chemically inert and resistant to corrosion, making them suitable for use in harsh environments.

5. **Electrical Properties:**

   a. Depending on composition, glassy materials can be insulating or semiconducting.

Applications of Glassy States

1. **Container and Packaging:**

   a. Used for bottles, jars, and containers due to their inertness and impermeability.

2. **Windows and Glazing:**

a. Common in architectural applications for their transparency and weather resistance.

3. Optical Devices:

a. Lenses, prisms, and optical fibers are made from glassy materials for use in cameras, microscopes, and telecommunications.

4. Electronics:

a. Substrates, insulators, and displays in electronic devices such as smartphones, computers, and TVs.

5. Medical Devices:

a. Glassy materials are used in medical implants, laboratory equipment, and diagnostic devices.

6. Insulation:

a. Glass wool and foam are used for thermal and acoustic insulation in buildings and appliances.

Challenges and Considerations

1. **Brittleness:** Glassy materials are prone to fracture under mechanical stress, limiting their use in load-bearing applications.

2. **Processing:** Fabricating glassy materials often requires specialized techniques such as casting, blowing, or extrusion.

3. **Cost:** Depending on composition and processing, glassy materials can be more expensive than alternative materials.

4. **Environmental Impact:** Some glassy materials may have significant energy and resource requirements for production, raising environmental concerns.

SOLID-CRYSTALLINE

Solid-crystalline states represent a highly ordered arrangement of atoms or molecules in a three-dimensional lattice structure. Crystalline solids exhibit distinct properties, including long-range order, periodicity, and well-defined crystallographic planes. Understanding the properties and characteristics of crystalline solids is fundamental in various scientific and industrial fields. Let's delve into solid-crystalline states in detail, including their properties and significance.

Definition:

Crystalline solids are a state of matter characterized by a highly ordered, repeating arrangement of atoms or molecules in a three-dimensional lattice structure.

Characteristics:

1. **Long-Range Order**: Crystalline solids have a regular, repeating pattern of atomic or molecular arrangement that extends throughout the material.

2. **Periodicity**: The arrangement of atoms or molecules in a crystalline solid follows specific crystallographic planes and directions.

3. **Sharp Melting Point:** Crystalline solids typically have a well-defined melting point at which they transition to the liquid state.

4. **Anisotropy**: Crystalline solids may exhibit different properties along different crystallographic axes due to their ordered structure.

Types of Crystalline Solids

1. **Ionic Crystals:**

    a. Composed of positively and negatively charged ions held together by electrostatic forces.

    b. Examples include sodium chloride (NaCl) and calcium fluoride (CaF_2).

2. **Covalent Crystals:**

    a. Formed by covalent bonds between atoms.

    b. Examples include diamond (carbon) and silicon dioxide (quartz).

3. **Metallic Crystals:**

    a. Composed of metal atoms held together by metallic bonding.

    b. Examples include iron (Fe), copper (Cu), and aluminum (Al).

4. **Molecular Crystals:**

a. Consist of discrete molecules held together by intermolecular forces.

b. Examples include ice (water) and sulfur.

Properties of Crystalline Solids

1. Mechanical Properties:

a. Crystalline solids can exhibit a wide range of mechanical properties, including hardness, brittleness, elasticity, and plasticity.

b. These properties depend on factors such as the type of bonding, crystal structure, and defect density.

2. Thermal Properties:

a. Crystalline solids have characteristic thermal conductivity, specific heat capacity, and thermal expansion coefficients.

b. These properties influence heat transfer, thermal stability, and temperature-dependent behavior.

3. Optical Properties:

a. Crystalline solids may be transparent, translucent, or opaque, depending on their molecular structure and electronic properties.

b. Optical phenomena such as reflection, refraction, and absorption are observed in crystalline materials.

4. Electrical Properties:

a. Crystalline solids can exhibit a wide range of electrical conductivity, from insulating to semiconducting to metallic.

b. These properties are determined by the band structure, electronic configuration, and defect density within the crystal lattice.

5. Magnetic Properties:

a. Some crystalline solids exhibit ferromagnetic, antiferromagnetic, or ferrimagnetic behavior due to the alignment of magnetic moments within the crystal lattice.

Applications of Crystalline Solids

1. **Semiconductors and Electronics:**

   a. Crystalline silicon and other semiconductor materials are used in integrated circuits, transistors, and photovoltaic devices.

2. **Construction and Engineering:**

   a. Crystalline materials such as metals and ceramics are used in structural components, building materials, and infrastructure.

3. **Jewelry and Gemstones:**

   a. Crystalline gems such as diamond, ruby, and sapphire are prized for their beauty, durability, and optical properties.

4. **Pharmaceuticals and Chemistry:**

   a. Many drugs and chemical compounds are crystalline solids, with properties that influence their solubility, stability, and bioavailability.

5. **Optics and Photonics:**

   a. Crystalline materials are used in lenses, mirrors, prisms, and optical fibers for applications in imaging, telecommunications, and laser technology.

6. **Energy Storage and Conversion:**

   a. Crystalline materials play a role in energy storage devices such as batteries and fuel cells, as well as in catalysis and energy conversion processes.

Challenges and Considerations

1. **Defects and Imperfections**: Crystal defects such as vacancies, dislocations, and grain boundaries can affect the mechanical, electrical, and optical properties of crystalline solids.

2. **Processing and Fabrication**: Producing large, defect-free crystalline materials often requires precise control over growth conditions, purification techniques, and processing parameters.

3. **Environmental Impact**: The extraction, processing, and disposal of crystalline materials can have environmental consequences, including resource depletion and pollution.

AMORPHOUS

Amorphous solids represent a unique phase of matter characterized by the absence of long-range order in their atomic or molecular arrangement. Unlike crystalline solids, which exhibit a highly ordered and repeating lattice structure, amorphous solids lack a regular pattern of atomic or molecular organization. Understanding the properties and behavior of amorphous states is crucial in various scientific, industrial, and technological applications. Let's explore amorphous states in detail, including their properties and significance.

Definition:

Amorphous solids are a state of matter characterized by the absence of long-range order in the arrangement of atoms or molecules. Instead of a repeating and regular lattice structure typical of crystalline solids, amorphous solids have a disordered and random atomic arrangement.

Characteristics:

1. **Lack of Long-Range Order**: Amorphous solids lack a repeating pattern of atomic or molecular arrangement extending throughout the material.

2. **Isotropic Properties:** Properties such as mechanical strength, thermal conductivity, and optical behavior are typically isotropic, meaning they are the same in all directions.

3. **Variability:** Amorphous solids can exhibit a wide range of properties depending on factors such as composition, processing conditions, and thermal history.

4. **Formation**: They are often formed by rapid cooling of a liquid or vapor, preventing the formation of a regular crystalline structure.

Types of Amorphous Solids

1. **Glasses:**

a. The most common type of amorphous solid, glasses are formed by the rapid cooling of a liquid below its glass transition temperature.

b. Examples include silica glass, borosilicate glass, and metallic glasses.

2. **Polymers:**

a. Many polymers exhibit an amorphous structure due to the random arrangement of polymer chains.

b. Examples include polystyrene, polyethylene, and polypropylene.

3. **Amorphous Metals:**

a. Also known as metallic glasses, these materials are formed by rapid solidification techniques, resulting in an amorphous atomic arrangement.

b. Examples include bulk metallic glasses (BMGs) and thin film metallic glasses.

4. **Amorphous Semiconductors:**

a. Certain semiconductor materials can exhibit an amorphous structure, offering unique electronic and optical properties.

b. Examples include hydrogenated amorphous silicon (a-Si:H) and amorphous selenium (a-Se).

Properties of Amorphous Solids

1. **Mechanical Properties:**

a. Amorphous solids can exhibit a wide range of mechanical properties, including hardness, elasticity, toughness, and ductility.

b. These properties are influenced by factors such as composition, molecular structure, and processing conditions.

2. **Thermal Properties:**

a. Amorphous solids typically have lower thermal conductivity compared to crystalline solids due to the lack of a regular atomic arrangement.

b. They may exhibit broad glass transition temperature ranges instead of sharp melting points.

3. Optical Properties:

a. Amorphous materials can be transparent, translucent, or opaque, depending on their composition and microstructure.

b. They may exhibit optical phenomena such as scattering, absorption, and fluorescence.

4. Electrical Properties:

a. Amorphous solids can be insulating, semiconducting, or metallic depending on their composition and electronic structure.

b. They find applications in electronic devices, photovoltaics, and sensors.

Applications of Amorphous Solids

1. Glassmaking and Ceramics:

a. Glasses are used in windows, bottles, optical fibers, and electronic displays.

2. Packaging and Containers:

a. Amorphous polymers are used in packaging films, containers, and consumer goods.

3. Electronics and Photonics:

a. Amorphous semiconductors find applications in thin-film transistors, solar cells, and sensors.

4. Medical Devices and Biomaterials:

a. Amorphous metals and polymers are used in medical implants, drug delivery systems, and tissue engineering.

5. Coatings and Protective Layers:

a. Metallic glasses are used as protective coatings, corrosion-resistant layers, and wear-resistant surfaces.

Challenges and Considerations

1. **Processing and Stability**: Producing amorphous solids with specific properties often requires precise control over processing parameters, such as cooling rate and composition.

2. **Structural Relaxation**: Amorphous solids may undergo structural relaxation over time, leading to changes in properties such as density, volume, and mechanical strength.

3. **Property Variability**: The properties of amorphous solids can vary significantly depending on factors such as composition, microstructure, and thermal history.

4. **Brittleness:** Amorphous solids can be brittle and prone to fracture under mechanical stress, limiting their use in load-bearing applications.

POLYMORPHISM

Polymorphism is a phenomenon observed in certain materials where a substance can exist in multiple crystalline forms or phases, each with distinct atomic or molecular arrangements. These different forms, known as polymorphs, have varying physical, chemical, and mechanical properties despite being composed of the same elements or molecules. Polymorphism is a crucial concept in materials science, pharmaceuticals, and various industrial applications. Let's explore polymorphism in detail, including its properties and significance.

Definition:

Polymorphism refers to the ability of a substance to exist in multiple crystalline forms or structures, each with its own unique arrangement of atoms or molecules.

Characteristics:

1. **Multiple Forms:** Polymorphic materials can exhibit two or more distinct crystal structures under different conditions of temperature, pressure, or composition.

2. **Different Properties**: Despite having the same chemical composition, polymorphs can have different physical, chemical, and mechanical properties, including density, melting point, solubility, and stability.

3. **Reversibility**: Polymorphic transformations can be reversible, meaning a substance can transition between different polymorphic forms under appropriate conditions.

Types of Polymorphism

1. **Allotropic Polymorphism:**

   a. Allotropy refers to polymorphism observed in elements, where different crystal structures arise due to variations in bonding or coordination environments.

   b. Examples include diamond and graphite (carbon allotropes) and iron (α-iron and γ-iron allotropes).

2. **Molecular Polymorphism:**

   a. Molecular compounds can exhibit polymorphism due to variations in packing arrangements or molecular conformations.

   b. Examples include polymorphic forms of organic molecules, such as pharmaceuticals and pigments.

3. **Ionic Polymorphism:**

   a. Ionic compounds may exhibit polymorphism based on variations in the arrangement of ions within the crystal lattice.

   b. Examples include polymorphic forms of salts and inorganic compounds.

Properties of Polymorphs

1. **Physical Properties:**

   a. Polymorphs can have different densities, crystal structures, melting points, and thermal expansion coefficients.

   b. These differences arise from variations in atomic or molecular arrangements within the crystal lattice.

2. **Chemical Properties:**

   a. Polymorphs may exhibit different chemical reactivities, solubilities, and dissolution rates due to differences in surface energies and crystal packing.

3. **Mechanical Properties:**

   a. Polymorphs can have different mechanical properties, including hardness, elasticity, and brittleness, depending on crystal structure and bonding interactions.

4. **Thermal Properties:**

   a. Different polymorphs may have distinct thermal conductivities, specific heat capacities, and thermal expansion behaviors.

Significance of Polymorphism

1. **Drug Development:**

   a. Polymorphism is critical in pharmaceuticals, where different polymorphs of a drug compound can exhibit varying bioavailability, solubility, and stability.

   b. Understanding and controlling polymorphism are essential for drug formulation, development, and regulatory approval.

2. **Materials Engineering:**

   a. Polymorphism offers opportunities to tailor material properties for specific applications, such as optimizing mechanical strength, thermal conductivity, or optical transparency.

3. **Crystallography and Solid-State Chemistry:**

   a. Studying polymorphism provides insights into crystallographic principles, intermolecular interactions, and phase transitions in materials science and chemistry.

4. **Industrial Processes:**

a. Polymorphism can affect manufacturing processes, product quality, and stability in industries such as food, cosmetics, and agrochemicals.

5. Biological Systems:

a. Polymorphism is observed in biological molecules and structures, such as proteins and DNA, influencing their structure, function, and interactions.

Challenges and Considerations

1. **Characterization**: Identifying and characterizing polymorphic forms require sophisticated analytical techniques such as X-ray diffraction, thermal analysis, and spectroscopy.

2. **Control:** Controlling polymorphism during synthesis, processing, and storage is crucial to ensuring product consistency and performance.

3. **Patents and Intellectual Property:** Polymorphism can have implications for patent protection and intellectual property rights, especially in the pharmaceutical industry.

Multiple Choice Questions (MCQs)

1. What is matter?

    A. Anything that occupies space and has no mass.

    B. Anything that has mass and does not occupy space.

    C. Anything that has mass and occupies space.

    D. Anything that has neither mass nor occupies space.

2. How many fundamental states of matter are generally recognized?

    A. Two

    B. Three

    C. Four

    D. Five

3. Which state of matter has a definite volume but an indefinite shape?

    A. Solid

    B. Liquid

    C. Gas

    D. Plasma

4. Which property is not a characteristic of a solid state?

    A. Definite volume

    B. Indefinite shape

    C. Definite shape

    D. High density

5. What causes gases to be highly compressible?

    A. High density

    B. Strong intermolecular forces

    C. Low density and large space between particles

    D. Low energy of particles

6. Which is not a characteristic of plasma?

    A. Conducts electricity

    B. Consists of neutral atoms

    C. Responds to magnetic fields

    D. Has high energy particles

7. What is viscosity a measure of in liquids?

    A. Transparency

    B. Compressibility

    C. Resistance to flow

    D. Ability to expand

8. Boyle's Law states that the pressure of a gas is inversely proportional to its:

    A. Temperature

    B. Volume

    C. Density

D. Mass

9. What is sublimation?

    A. Transition from solid to liquid

    B. Transition from gas to liquid

    C. Transition from liquid to gas

    D. Transition from solid to gas without passing through the liquid state

10. Which property is most associated with the behavior of gases under different conditions?

    A. Viscosity

    B. Pressure

    C. Surface tension

    D. Capillary action

11. Latent heat of fusion is the energy required for a substance to:

    A. Change from gas to liquid

    B. Change from liquid to gas

    C. Change from solid to gas

    D. Change from solid to liquid

12. Which is a chemical property of matter?

    A. Melting point

    B. Density

    C. Flammability

    D. Volume

13. What is the critical point in the context of states of matter?

    A. The temperature at which a solid becomes a gas

    B. The point where solid, liquid, and gas phases coexist

    C. The end point of the phase equilibrium curve between liquid and gas

    D. The highest temperature at which a substance can exist as a liquid under any pressure

14. Eutectic mixtures are characterized by having:

A. The same melting point as pure components

B. Higher melting points than any of the components

C. Lower melting points than any of the components

D. Variable melting points based on pressure

15. What does the Clausius-Clapeyron equation describe?

A. The relationship between the states of matter

B. The relationship between vapour pressure and temperature

C. The process of sublimation

D. The changes in the kinetic energy of particles

16. What role do aerosols play in medical inhalers?

A. They stabilize the medication

B. They create a suspension of medication in a gas for delivery

C. They act as a propellant to expel the medication

D. They decrease the medication's effectiveness

17. Relative humidity measures:

A. The total amount of water vapor in the air

B. The ratio of current water vapor in the air to the maximum amount it
can hold at that temperature

C. The dew point temperature

D. The absolute humidity level

18. What is meant by 'amorphous' in materials science?

A. Materials with a well-ordered crystalline structure

B. Materials that are semi-crystalline

C. Materials without a long-range order

D. Materials with a single crystal form

19. Which state of matter is characterized by having an indefinite shape and
volume?

A. Solid

B. Liquid

C. Gas

D. Plasma

20. What is the significance of polymorphism in pharmaceuticals?

    A. It affects the color and taste of drugs

    B. It affects the solubility and stability of drugs

    C. It affects the size and shape of drugs

    D. It affects the thermal properties of drugs

Short Answer Type Questions (Subjective)

1. What defines a substance as matter?

2. Describe the primary difference between a solid and a liquid state of matter.

3. What is viscosity and how is it significant in liquids?

4. Explain Boyle's Law and its importance in understanding gas behavior.

5. What is plasma and where can it commonly be found?

6. Define sublimation with an example of a material that undergoes this process.

7. What are physical properties of matter? Provide two examples.

8. Describe a chemical property of matter with an example.

9. What does the Clausius-Clapeyron equation describe?

10. How do aerosols function in medical inhalers?

11. Explain the significance of relative humidity in weather prediction.

12. What is the critical point in the context of states of matter?

13. Describe what a eutectic mixture is and give an example.

14. What role do intermolecular forces play in determining the state of matter?

15. How does the latent heat of fusion differ from the latent heat of vaporization?

16. What is meant by amorphous in the context of material science?

17. Explain how pressure and temperature influence vapor pressure.

18. What is the importance of the melting point in understanding solid substances?

19. Describe how changes in volume and temperature are related under Charles's Law.

20. What is polymorphism in materials science, and why is it significant?

Long Answer Type Questions (Subjective)

1. Discuss the four fundamental states of matter and their characteristics. Include examples for each state.

2. Explain how the properties of gases are influenced by changes in temperature and pressure according to the ideal gas law.

3. Describe the process and significance of sublimation and deposition in the phase transitions of matter. Include relevant examples.

4. Detail the application and importance of latent heats in industrial and natural processes.

5. How does vapor pressure affect the boiling point of a liquid? Explain with the concept of normal and high-altitude boiling points.

6. Discuss the role of eutectic mixtures in industrial applications and natural processes.

7. Explain how liquid crystals work and their applications in modern technology.

8. Detail the formation and properties of amorphous solids, and discuss their applications in various industries.

9. Describe the phenomenon of polymorphism and its implications in pharmaceuticals and materials science.

10. Explain the critical point and its significance in creating supercritical fluids, including applications in various fields.

Answer Key

1. (C) Anything that has mass and occupies space.

2. (C) Four

3. (B) Liquid

4. (B) Indefinite shape

5. (C) Low density and large space between particles

6. (B) Consists of neutral atoms

7. (C) Resistance to flow

8. (B) Volume

9. (D) Transition from solid to gas without passing through the liquid state

10.(B) Pressure

11.(D) Change from solid to liquid

12.(C) Flammability

13.(C) The end point of the phase equilibrium curve between liquid and gas

14.(C) Lower melting points than any of the components

15.(B) The relationship between vapour pressure and temperature

16.(B) They create a suspension of medication in a gas for delivery

17.(B) The ratio of current water vapor in the air to the maximum amount it can hold at that temperature

18.(C) Materials without a long-range order

19.(D) Plasma

20.(B) It affects the solubility and stability of drugs

CHAPTER – 3

PHYSICOCHEMICAL PROPERTIES OF DRUG MOLECULES

Physicochemical properties of drug molecules refer to their physical and chemical characteristics that influence their behavior within biological systems. These properties play a crucial role in drug design, formulation, absorption, distribution, metabolism, and excretion (ADME). Some important physicochemical properties include:

1. **Solubility:** The ability of a drug to dissolve in a solvent, typically water. Solubility impacts the drug's absorption and bioavailability.

2. **Lipophilicity/Hydrophobicity:** The tendency of a drug molecule to dissolve in fats (lipids) or water. Lipophilic drugs tend to cross cell membranes more easily but might have issues with solubility in aqueous environments.

3. **Molecular Size and Shape:** Larger molecules might have difficulty passing through biological barriers, affecting their absorption and distribution within the body.

4. **Ionization State**: The ionization of a drug affects its solubility and ability to cross membranes since ionized forms might have different properties than non-ionized ones.

5. **Chemical Stability:** The susceptibility of a drug to undergo chemical changes, such as degradation or decomposition, which can affect its efficacy and safety.

6. **Partition Coefficient (Log P):** A measure of the lipophilicity of a compound, often used to predict its ability to pass through biological membranes.

7. **Melting Point and Boiling Point:** These properties can influence the formulation of drugs for oral administration, injectables, or topical use.

8. **Polarity:** Determines the interaction of a drug molecule with polar solvents or biological structures. Polar drugs may have different distribution and elimination patterns compared to non-polar ones.

REFRACTIVE INDEX

The refractive index (RI) of a substance is a measure of how much the speed of light is reduced or refracted when it passes through that substance compared to its speed in a vacuum. Mathematically, it's the ratio of the speed of light in a vacuum to the speed of light in the substance.

The formula for refractive index (n) is:

$$n=c/v$$

Where:

n = Refractive index

c = Speed of light in a vacuum

v = Speed of light in the substance

The refractive index can provide valuable information about the optical properties and composition of a material. It's used in various fields, including:

a. **Optics:** In determining the behavior of light passing through different materials, like lenses, prisms, or fiber optics.

b. **Chemistry and Material Science:** The refractive index can be used to identify and characterize substances, especially in conjunction with other analytical techniques.

c. **Pharmaceuticals:** It's used in quality control to identify and authenticate drug compounds based on their refractive properties.

d. **Geology:** Helps in identifying minerals and their composition.

e. **Physics:** It's a critical parameter in understanding the interaction of light with matter.

OPTICAL ROTATION

Optical rotation is a phenomenon observed when polarized light passes through certain substances, causing the plane of polarization to rotate. This rotation occurs due to the interaction of polarized light with chiral molecules, which are molecules that lack a plane of symmetry and exist in two non-superimposable mirror image forms (enantiomers).

Key points about optical rotation:

1. **Chirality:** Chiral molecules have two enantiomeric forms (mirror images that cannot be superimposed on each other). This property is essential for optical rotation.

2. **Polarized Light:** Light that oscillates in one plane is called polarized light. When polarized light passes through a chiral substance, the plane of polarization rotates.

3. **Specific Rotation:** The amount of rotation is quantified by a parameter called specific rotation ($[\alpha]$). It's a characteristic property of a substance at a specific temperature, concentration, and wavelength of light. The formula is:

$$[\alpha] = \alpha/lc$$

Where:

   a. $[\alpha]$ = Specific rotation
   b. α = Observed rotation in degrees
   c. l = Path length of the sample in decimeters
   d. c = Concentration of the substance in grams per milliliter

4. **Measurement:** A polarimeter is used to measure optical rotation. It consists of a light source, polarizer, sample cell, and analyzer. By measuring the angle of rotation, the specific rotation of a compound can be determined.

5. **Applications:** Optical rotation is crucial in identifying and characterizing chiral compounds, such as pharmaceuticals, flavors, and fragrances. Enantiomers often exhibit different biological activities, so understanding their specific rotations is important in drug development to ensure the right form is used for efficacy and safety.

6. **Racemic Mixtures**: A racemic mixture contains equal amounts of both enantiomers and typically exhibits no net optical rotation because the rotations cancel each other out.

In pharmaceuticals, optical rotation measurements help determine the purity, identity, and concentration of chiral drug substances, ensuring the right form is used in formulations to achieve the desired therapeutic effect.

DIELECTRIC CONSTANT

The dielectric constant, also known as the relative permittivity, is a measure of a material's ability to store electrical energy in an electric field. It's the ratio of the permittivity of a substance to the permittivity of free space (a vacuum).

Permittivity is a measure of how much electric field a material can permit or allow to pass through it. It determines how an electric field affects and interacts with the atoms and molecules within a substance.

Mathematically, the dielectric constant (εr) is given by:

$$\varepsilon r = \varepsilon 0 / \varepsilon$$

Where:

εr = Dielectric constant or relative permittivity

ε = Permittivity of the material

$\varepsilon 0$ = Permittivity of free space (vacuum)

Key points about the dielectric constant:

1. **Effect on Electric Fields:** Materials with a higher dielectric constant have greater ability to store electrical energy in an electric field.

2. **Electrical Insulation:** Dielectric materials are often used as insulators in capacitors and electrical components. They help prevent the flow of electrical current while allowing the storage of electric charge.

3. **Polarization:** Dielectric materials can become polarized when subjected to an electric field. This polarization contributes to their ability to store energy and affects the overall electric field in the material.

4. **Frequency Dependence:** The dielectric constant of a material can vary with frequency. At different frequencies, materials may exhibit different dielectric constants due to factors like molecular structure and polarization mechanisms.

5. **Applications:** Dielectric constants are important in various fields, including electrical engineering, electronics, material science, and chemistry. They are fundamental in designing and understanding the behavior of capacitors, transmission lines, insulators, and other electrical devices.

In pharmaceuticals and chemistry, knowledge of the dielectric constant of solvents is crucial in various processes such as dissolution, extraction, and formulation, as it can affect the solubility and behavior of substances in those solvents.

DIPOLE MOMENT

The dipole moment is a measure of the polarity or the distribution of charge within a molecule. It quantifies the separation of positive and negative charges within a molecule due to differences in electronegativity or molecular structure.

Here are some key points about the dipole moment:

1. **Definition:** The dipole moment (μ) is a vector quantity defined as the product of the magnitude of the charge (q) and the distance (d) between the charges in a molecule: $\mu = q \times d$ The direction of the dipole moment points from the negative to the positive charge.

2. **Polarity:** A molecule with a non-uniform distribution of electrons, where one end is more electronegative (having a higher electron density) and the other end is less electronegative, will have a dipole moment. Polar molecules have a non-zero dipole moment.

3. **Measurement:** The dipole moment is measured in Debye units (D), where 1 Debye is approximately 3.336×10^{-30} C·m (coulomb-meter).

4. **Factors Influencing Dipole Moment:**

    a. **Electronegativity:** Greater electronegativity difference between atoms in a molecule leads to a larger dipole moment.

    b. **Molecular Geometry:** Asymmetrical or non-linear molecular shapes often result in a non-zero dipole moment.

5. **Importance:** Dipole moments are crucial in understanding the behavior of molecules in various fields, including chemistry, biology, and material science. They influence properties such as solubility, boiling point, and intermolecular interactions.

6. **Applications:** In pharmaceuticals, knowledge of the dipole moment of molecules is valuable for understanding drug-receptor interactions, drug solubility in biological systems, and the design of new drugs with specific properties.

The dipole moment provides insight into the overall polarity of a molecule and is a key concept in understanding the interactions between molecules in a variety of chemical and biological processes.

DISSOCIATION CONSTANT

The dissociation constant, often denoted as Kdissociation or simply Kd, is a measure used in chemistry to describe the extent of dissociation or the equilibrium between a compound and its dissociated components in a solution.

For a generic equilibrium reaction between a compound (A) and its dissociated components (B and C):

$$A \rightleftharpoons B+C$$

$$A \rightleftharpoons B+C$$

The dissociation constant is defined as the ratio of the concentration of the dissociated products (B and C) to the concentration of the undissociated compound (A) at equilibrium:

$$Kd=[B]\times[C]/[A]$$

Where:

Kd= Dissociation constant

$[X]$ = Concentration of species X

In the context of acids and bases, dissociation constants are commonly used to describe the extent of ionization in aqueous solutions. For example:

a. **Acid Dissociation Constant (Ka):** Describes the extent of dissociation of an acid into its conjugate base and a proton in solution.

b. **Base Dissociation Constant (Kb):** Describes the extent of dissociation of a base into its conjugate acid and hydroxide ions in solution.

These constants help determine the strength of acids and bases:

1. Strong acids or bases have high dissociation constants, indicating complete or almost complete dissociation in solution.

2. Weak acids or bases have lower dissociation constants, indicating partial dissociation, and they establish an equilibrium between the undissociated and dissociated forms.

In pharmaceuticals and biochemistry, understanding dissociation constants is crucial in drug development, particularly when considering drug-receptor interactions, determining drug solubility, and predicting the behavior of drugs in physiological environments. It helps in optimizing drug formulations and assessing the efficacy of pharmaceutical compounds.

DETERMINATIONS AND APPLICATIONS

Determinations and applications in the context of chemistry and pharmaceuticals cover a broad range of techniques, measurements, and analyses. Here's a breakdown of key determinations and their applications:

Determinations:

1. **Quantitative Analysis:** Determination of quantities or concentrations of substances in a sample using various analytical techniques such as titration, spectrophotometry, chromatography, and mass spectrometry.

2. **Physical Properties:** Determination of physical characteristics like melting point, boiling point, density, refractive index, and solubility of substances. These properties aid in substance identification and characterization.

3. **Chemical Properties:** Determination of chemical reactivity, stability, and kinetics of reactions, essential in understanding the behavior of substances in various environments and formulations.

4. **Kinetics and Thermodynamics:** Determination of reaction rates, equilibrium constants, activation energies, enthalpy, and entropy changes in chemical reactions. This information is vital in designing and optimizing chemical processes.

Applications:

1. **Pharmaceutical Formulation:** Determinations of solubility, stability, and compatibility of drug substances with excipients, aiding in the development of effective and stable drug formulations.

2. **Quality Control:** Determinations of purity, potency, and concentrations of active pharmaceutical ingredients (APIs) in drug products to ensure they meet regulatory standards and are safe for consumption.

3. **Drug-Target Interactions:** Determinations of binding affinities, dissociation constants, and kinetics of drug-receptor interactions are crucial in drug discovery and development to design more effective and specific medications.

4. **Environmental Analysis:** Determinations of pollutant concentrations, toxicity levels, and degradation rates of chemicals to assess environmental impacts and develop remediation strategies.

5. **Material Science:** Determinations of properties such as strength, conductivity, and durability of materials for various applications in engineering, electronics, and construction.

6. **Biological Studies:** Determinations of biomolecular structures, enzymatic activity, and metabolic pathways aid in understanding biological processes, disease mechanisms, and potential therapeutic targets.

These determinations and applications collectively contribute to advancing scientific knowledge, enabling the development of new materials, drugs, technologies, and environmental solutions. They play a pivotal role across scientific disciplines and industries, fostering innovation and problem-solving in diverse fields.

Multiple-Choice Questions (Mcqs):

1. What physicochemical property of drug molecules significantly impacts their absorption and bioavailability?
   a) Molecular Size and Shape
   b) Melting Point
   c) Refractive Index
   d) Chemical Stability

2. Optical rotation occurs due to the interaction of polarized light with:
   a) Linear molecules
   b) Chiral molecules
   c) Symmetrical molecules
   d) Non-polar molecules

3. The specific rotation of a substance is determined by:
   a) Path length and concentration

b) Wavelength and temperature

c) Concentration and solvent polarity

d) Molecular weight and structure

4. Which property measures a material's ability to store electrical energy in an electric field?

   a) Refractive Index

   b) Dipole Moment

   c) Dielectric Constant

   d) Dissociation Constant

5. In a molecule, a non-zero dipole moment indicates:

   a) Symmetry

   b) Polar nature

   c) Non-polar nature

   d) Aromaticity

6. The dielectric constant is a measure of a material's ability to:

   a) Conduct electricity

   b) Store electrical energy

   c) Resist temperature changes

   d) Resist chemical reactions

7. What factor influences the dipole moment of a molecule?

   a) Molecular weight

   b) Temperature

   c) Molecular geometry

   d) Refractive index

8. The dissociation constant describes:

   a) The extent of ionization in a solution

   b) The strength of intermolecular forces

   c) The solubility of a substance

   d) The reaction rate of a compound

9. Which constant measures the extent of dissociation of an acid in solution?

    a) Ka (Acid Dissociation Constant)

    b) Kb (Base Dissociation Constant)

    c) Ksp (Solubility Product Constant)

    d) Keq (Equilibrium Constant)

10. What does a racemic mixture contain?

    a) Two identical enantiomers

    b) Two different enantiomers

    c) Only one enantiomer

    d) No enantiomers

11. What tool is commonly used to measure optical rotation?

    a) Spectrophotometer

    b) Polarimeter

    c) Refractometer

    d) Microscope

12. Which property determines the interaction of a drug molecule with polar solvents or biological structures?

    a) Melting Point

    b) Lipophilicity

    c) Refractive Index

    d) Solubility

13. Which of the following is NOT a physicochemical property of drug molecules?

    a) Specific Rotation

    b) Dipole Moment

    c) Boiling Point

    d) Dissociation Constant

14. The dipole moment of a molecule increases with:

    a) Increased electronegativity difference

b) Symmetrical structure

c) Decreased molecular weight

d) Non-polar nature

15. Dielectric materials are commonly used as:

a) Conductors

b) Insulators

c) Semiconductors

d) Superconductors

16. What determines the behavior of molecules in various fields such as chemistry, biology, and material science?

a) Dipole Moment

b) Refractive Index

c) Specific Rotation

d) Dielectric Constant

17. The dissociation constant is a measure used to describe:

a) Molecular weight

b) Acid strength

c) Polarizability

d) Ionic conductivity

18. What is the importance of measuring the dipole moment of molecules?

a) Determines color properties

b) Predicts boiling point

c) Understands solubility

d) Predicts intermolecular interactions

19. What does a higher dielectric constant indicate about a material?

a) Lower electrical resistance

b) Higher electrical conductivity

c) Greater ability to store electrical energy

d) Reduced polarization

20.What do optical rotation measurements assist in identifying and characterizing in pharmaceuticals?

    a) Molecular weight

    b) Chiral compounds

    c) Refractive index

    d) Dielectric constant

Short Answer Type Questions:

1. Define solubility and explain its significance in drug absorption.

2. What is specific rotation, and how is it measured in a polarimeter?

3. Describe the role of chiral molecules in optical rotation and their importance in pharmaceuticals.

4. Explain the concept of the dielectric constant and its relevance in pharmaceutical processes.

5. Define the dipole moment and discuss its influence on molecular behavior in chemistry and biology.

6. What is the dissociation constant, and how does it aid in understanding acids and bases?

7. Enumerate the key determinations in pharmaceutical formulation and their significance.

8. How does the refractive index contribute to identifying substances in pharmaceutical quality control?

9. Discuss the applications of dielectric constants in various scientific fields.

10.Explain the significance of physical and chemical properties in substance identification and characterization.

Long Answer Type Questions:

1. Discuss the impact of molecular size, shape, and polarity on a drug molecule's behavior within biological systems, emphasizing their role in pharmacokinetics.

2. Explain the principles of optical rotation and its applications in characterizing chiral compounds in pharmaceuticals, flavors, and fragrances. Provide examples.

3. Elaborate on the role of the dielectric constant in pharmaceutical processes, highlighting its influence on solubility, dissolution, and formulation.

4. Compare and contrast the concepts of specific rotation and refractive index in identifying and characterizing substances in pharmaceutical quality control.

5. Discuss the significance of dipole moments in understanding molecular interactions and their relevance in drug-receptor interactions in pharmaceuticals.

6. Explain the applications of dissociation constants in determining drug solubility, optimizing formulations, and predicting drug behavior in physiological environments.

7. Analyze the role of various determinations in pharmaceutical formulation, elucidating their impact on the development of stable and effective drug formulations.

8. Detail the applications of dielectric constants across fields such as electrical engineering, material science, and pharmaceuticals, highlighting their diverse significance.

9. Discuss the interplay between physical and chemical properties in substance identification, characterization, and their impact on drug design and development.

10.Explore the comprehensive role of determinations and applications in advancing scientific knowledge, fostering innovation, and problem-solving across multiple scientific disciplines and industries.

Answer key:

1. a) Molecular Size and Shape

2. b) Chiral molecules

3. a) Path length and concentration

4. c) Dielectric Constant

5. b) Polar nature

6. b) Store electrical energy

7. c) Molecular geometry

8. a) The extent of ionization in a solution

9. a) Ka (Acid Dissociation Constant)

10.b) Two different enantiomers

11.b) Polarimeter

12.b) Lipophilicity

13.d) Dissociation Constant

14.a) Increased electronegativity difference

15.b) Insulators

16.a) Dipole Moment

17.b) Acid strength

18.d) Predicts intermolecular interactions

19.c) Greater ability to store electrical energy

20.b) Chiral compounds

CHAPTER – 4

SURFACE AND INTERFACIAL PHENOMENON

INTRODUCTION:

Surface and interfacial phenomena encompass the study of physical and chemical behaviors that occur at the interfaces of different phases, such as solid-liquid, liquid-liquid, liquid-gas, and solid-gas interfaces. These phenomena are crucial in a wide range of scientific and industrial processes, including coatings, detergency, emulsions, catalysis, and biological systems.

Key Concepts

1. **Surface Tension and Interfacial Tension:**
    a. **Surface Tension:** This is the energy or force that acts on the surface of a liquid, minimizing its area. It arises because molecules at the surface experience a net inward force, leading to a 'contractive' effect.
    b. **Interfacial Tension**: Similar to surface tension but occurs at the interface between two immiscible liquids, or a liquid and a solid, influencing phenomena like emulsion stability.

2. **Adsorption:**
    a. **Physical Adsorption (Physisorption):** Involves weak van der Waals forces and is usually reversible.
    b. **Chemical Adsorption (Chemisorption):** Involves the formation of strong chemical bonds, which can be either reversible or irreversible.

3. **Wettability and Contact Angle:**
    a. **Wettability:** The ability of a liquid to maintain contact with a solid surface, influenced by intermolecular interactions.
    b. **Contact Angle**: The angle at which a liquid-vapor interface meets a solid surface. It quantifies wettability and is affected by surface tension and interfacial forces.

4. **Capillarity:**
   a. Describes the ability of a liquid to flow in narrow spaces without the assistance of external forces, governed by the interaction between liquid and solid surfaces.

5. **Surfactants:**
   a. Surface-active agents that reduce surface and interfacial tension. They have a hydrophilic (water-attracting) head and a hydrophobic (water-repelling) tail, enabling them to stabilize emulsions and foams.

Applications

1. **Detergency and Cleaning:**
   a. Surfactants are crucial in detergents to lower surface tension and help remove dirt and oils from surfaces.

2. **Emulsions and Foams:**
   a. Emulsions are mixtures of two immiscible liquids stabilized by surfactants. Foams are gas-liquid interfaces stabilized similarly.

3. **Coating and Painting:**
   a. Surface and interfacial phenomena determine the adhesion and spreading of coatings on surfaces, impacting durability and finish quality.

4. **Biological Systems:**
   a. Cell membranes, protein folding, and enzyme activities are governed by interfacial interactions. Lipid bilayers, for example, form due to hydrophobic interactions at the molecular level.

5. **Catalysis:**
   a. Many catalytic reactions occur at solid-liquid or solid-gas interfaces, where the surface properties of the catalyst play a significant role in reaction rates and mechanisms.

LIQUID INTERFACE

Liquid interfaces play a pivotal role in surface and interfacial phenomena, particularly in contexts where liquids come into contact with other phases, such as gases, solids, or other immiscible liquids. These interfaces are fundamental in numerous natural processes and industrial applications. Here, we explore the liquid interfaces in detail, covering their properties, behaviors, and practical implications.

Key Properties of Liquid Interfaces

1. **Surface Tension:**
   a. Surface tension is the energy required to increase the surface area of a liquid due to the cohesive forces among molecules at the surface. Molecules at the liquid surface experience a net inward force, leading to minimized surface area and spherical shapes in droplets.
   b. Surface tension is typically measured in milliNewtons per meter (mN/m).

2. **Interfacial Tension:**
   a. Interfacial tension is similar to surface tension but occurs at the interface between two immiscible liquids. It results from the imbalance of intermolecular forces at the boundary.
   b. This tension affects the shape and stability of droplets and emulsions.

3. **Contact Angle and Wettability:**
   a. The contact angle is the angle formed at the junction of the liquid, solid, and gas phases. It quantifies the wettability of a surface by a liquid.
   b. A low contact angle indicates good wettability, meaning the liquid spreads easily over the surface, while a high contact angle indicates poor wettability.

4. **Capillarity:**
   a. Capillary action is the movement of liquid within narrow spaces without the assistance of external forces. This phenomenon is driven

by the adhesive forces between the liquid and solid surfaces and the cohesive forces within the liquid.

b. Capillary rise is an essential aspect of processes such as ink in pens and water uptake in plants.

Behaviors at Liquid Interfaces

1. Adsorption:

a. Molecules or particles at the liquid interface can be adsorbed from either phase. This adsorption can significantly alter the physical and chemical properties of the interface.

b. Surfactants are a prime example, adsorbing at interfaces to reduce surface and interfacial tension.

2. Marangoni Effect:

a. This effect involves mass transfer along an interface due to gradients in surface tension. These gradients can arise from temperature or concentration differences, causing fluid motion.

b. The Marangoni effect plays a role in processes like the spreading of liquids and the stability of foams and emulsions.

3. Emulsification:

a. Emulsification is the process of mixing two immiscible liquids to form an emulsion, with one liquid dispersed in the other in the form of droplets. Surfactants stabilize these droplets by reducing interfacial tension and preventing coalescence.

4. Practical Implications

5. Detergency and Cleaning:

a. Surfactants lower the surface tension of water, improving its ability to wet and penetrate soils and oils, facilitating their removal from surfaces during cleaning.

6. **Pharmaceuticals and Cosmetics:**
   a. Emulsions are crucial in formulating products like creams and lotions, where oil and water phases are mixed. The stability and texture of these products are directly related to the interfacial properties.

7. **Food Industry:**
   a. Emulsifiers are used to stabilize products like mayonnaise and salad dressings. The texture, stability, and appearance of these foods depend on the control of liquid interfaces.

8. **Enhanced Oil Recovery:**
   a. In petroleum engineering, surfactants are used to reduce the interfacial tension between oil and water, enhancing the extraction of oil from reservoirs.

9. **Biological Systems:**
   a. Cell membranes, composed of lipid bilayers, are a prime example of liquid-liquid interfaces. The behavior of these membranes is crucial for cell function, signaling, and transport.

SURFACE TENSIONS

Surface tension is a fundamental concept in surface and interfacial phenomena. It is the force that acts at the interface of a liquid and a gas, or between immiscible liquids, due to the cohesive forces among liquid molecules. Surface tension plays a critical role in various natural processes and industrial applications.

Definition and Origin

1. **Surface Tension:**
   a. Surface tension is the energy required to increase the surface area of a liquid by a unit area. It is typically measured in milliNewtons per meter (mN/m).
   b. It arises because molecules at the surface of a liquid experience a net inward cohesive force, which minimizes the surface area.

2. **Molecular Origin:**
   a. Inside the liquid, molecules are surrounded by other molecules and experience balanced forces in all directions.
   b. At the surface, molecules are not surrounded by like molecules on all sides, resulting in an inward force that creates surface tension.

Measurement of Surface Tension

1. **Capillary Rise Method:**
   a. A liquid rises or falls in a capillary tube due to surface tension. The height of the liquid column is used to calculate the surface tension using the Jurin's law.

2. **Drop Weight or Drop Volume Method:**
   a. Surface tension is determined by measuring the weight or volume of a droplet of liquid detaching from a nozzle.

3. **Tensiometer:**
   a. A tensiometer measures the force required to detach a ring or plate from the liquid surface, providing a direct measurement of surface tension.

4. **Wilhelmy Plate Method:**
   a. A thin plate is partially immersed in the liquid, and the force exerted on the plate is measured to calculate surface tension.

Factors Affecting Surface Tension

1. **Temperature:**
   a. Surface tension decreases with increasing temperature as thermal agitation reduces cohesive forces among surface molecules.

2. **Impurities and Surfactants:**
   a. Surfactants (surface-active agents) significantly reduce surface tension by concentrating at the surface and disrupting cohesive forces.
   b. Impurities can either increase or decrease surface tension, depending on their nature and concentration.

3. **Nature of Liquid:**

    a. Different liquids have different surface tensions based on their molecular interactions. For instance, water has a high surface tension due to strong hydrogen bonding.

Applications of Surface Tension

1. **Detergents and Cleaning:**

    - Surfactants in detergents lower the surface tension of water, enhancing its ability to wet surfaces and emulsify oils and dirt, making them easier to remove.

2. **Emulsions and Foams:**

    - Surface tension controls the formation and stability of emulsions and foams. Surfactants help stabilize these systems by reducing interfacial tension between immiscible liquids or gas-liquid interfaces.

3. **Capillary Action:**

    - Surface tension drives capillary action, enabling liquids to flow in narrow spaces. This phenomenon is critical in processes such as ink movement in pens and water transport in plants.

4. **Coatings and Adhesion:**

    - The wettability of surfaces, influenced by surface tension, is crucial in coatings, paints, and adhesives. Proper surface tension ensures good adhesion and uniform coating.

5. **Biological Processes:**

    - Surface tension is essential in many biological processes. For example, lung function relies on surfactants to reduce surface tension in the alveoli, preventing lung collapse.

Advanced Concepts

1. **Marangoni Effect:**

    a. This effect involves fluid motion driven by gradients in surface tension, caused by temperature or concentration differences. It plays a role in various natural and industrial processes, such as welding and crystal growth.

2. **Surface Energy:**

    a. Surface tension is related to surface energy, the excess energy at the surface of a material compared to its bulk. Surface energy determines the interactions at interfaces and the behavior of droplets on solid surfaces.

3. **Young-Laplace Equation:**

    a. This equation relates the pressure difference across a curved liquid interface to surface tension and the radius of curvature. It explains phenomena like bubble formation and droplet shapes.

INTERFACIAL TENSIONS

Interfacial tension is a crucial concept in the study of surface and interfacial phenomena. It describes the force per unit length existing at the interface between two immiscible phases, such as oil and water, and plays a significant role in various scientific and industrial processes.

Definition and Origin

1. **Interfacial Tension:**

    a. Interfacial tension is the energy required to increase the surface area of the interface between two immiscible liquids per unit area. It is typically measured in milliNewtons per meter (mN/m).

    b. It arises due to the imbalance of intermolecular forces at the interface. Molecules at the interface experience different interactions compared to those in the bulk phases, leading to the formation of an interface with distinct properties.

2. **Molecular Origin:**

    a. In the bulk of each liquid, molecules experience uniform attractive forces from neighboring molecules.

b. At the interface, molecules are subjected to different types of intermolecular forces from the two different phases, leading to an energetic penalty that manifests as interfacial tension.

Measurement of Interfacial Tension

1. Drop Shape Analysis:

a. The shape of a droplet of one liquid in another immiscible liquid is analyzed. The Young-Laplace equation relates the shape of the drop to the interfacial tension.

2. Pendant Drop Method:

a. A droplet of one liquid is suspended in another, and its shape is analyzed. The interfacial tension is determined based on the droplet's profile and the balance of forces acting on it.

3. Spinning Drop Method:

a. A drop of one liquid is placed inside a rotating tube filled with another liquid. The interfacial tension is calculated from the shape of the elongated drop formed due to centrifugal forces.

4. Wilhelmy Plate Method:

a. Similar to its use in measuring surface tension, a plate is immersed at the interface between two immiscible liquids, and the force acting on it is measured.

Factors Affecting Interfacial Tension

1. Temperature:

a. Interfacial tension generally decreases with increasing temperature as thermal motion reduces the cohesive forces at the interface.

2. Surfactants:

a. Surfactants can significantly reduce interfacial tension by adsorbing at the interface and disrupting the intermolecular forces. They are used to stabilize emulsions and foams.

3. Concentration of Solutes:

a. The presence of solutes can alter the interfacial tension depending on their affinity for the two phases involved. Solutes that preferentially partition into one phase can decrease interfacial tension.

4. **Nature of Liquids:**

   a. The chemical nature of the liquids, such as polarity and molecular structure, affects the interfacial tension. Immiscible liquids with similar molecular interactions tend to have lower interfacial tension.

Applications of Interfacial Tension

1. **Emulsions:**

   a. Interfacial tension plays a critical role in the formation and stability of emulsions, which are mixtures of two immiscible liquids. Reducing interfacial tension with surfactants helps create stable emulsions used in food, pharmaceuticals, and cosmetics.

2. **Enhanced Oil Recovery:**

   a. In petroleum engineering, reducing the interfacial tension between oil and water can enhance the extraction of oil from reservoirs. Surfactants are used to improve oil displacement efficiency.

3. **Detergency:**

   a. In cleaning applications, surfactants lower the interfacial tension between water and oily soils, facilitating the removal of dirt and grease from surfaces.

4. **Foam Stability:**

   a. The stability of foams, which are gas-liquid interfaces, is influenced by interfacial tension. Surfactants stabilize foams by reducing the interfacial tension, making them useful in various industrial processes.

5. **Biological Systems:**

a. Cell membranes and other biological interfaces have specific interfacial properties essential for functions like nutrient transport, signaling, and cellular structure.

Advanced Concepts

1. Young-Laplace Equation:

a. This equation describes the pressure difference across a curved interface as a function of the interfacial tension and the curvature of the interface. It is fundamental in understanding bubble and droplet formation.

2. Gibbs Adsorption Isotherm:

a. This relationship describes how the surface concentration of an adsorbate at an interface varies with its bulk concentration, influencing the interfacial tension.

3. Marangoni Effect:

a. The Marangoni effect involves mass transfer along an interface due to gradients in interfacial tension. These gradients can result from variations in temperature or concentration and can drive fluid motion.

SURFACE FREE ENERGY

Surface free energy is a fundamental concept in surface and interfacial phenomena, describing the energetic properties of a surface and its interactions with surrounding phases. It is crucial in understanding adhesion, wetting, and other surface-related processes.

Definition and Origin

1. Surface Free Energy:

a. Surface free energy (often denoted as γ) is the work required to create a unit area of a surface. It is a measure of the excess energy at the surface of a material compared to its bulk.

b. It arises because atoms or molecules at the surface of a material are not fully surrounded by other atoms or molecules, resulting in an imbalance of forces and higher energy state.

2. Molecular Origin:

a. In the bulk material, molecules experience uniform interactions with neighboring molecules.

b. At the surface, molecules are subject to fewer neighboring interactions, leading to higher energy states and the manifestation of surface free energy.

Measurement of Surface Free Energy

1. Contact Angle Measurements:

a. The contact angle (θ) formed by a liquid droplet on a solid surface is measured. The surface free energy can be estimated using Young's equation and related models like the Owens-Wendt or the Zisman method.

b. Young's Equation:

$$\gamma SV = \gamma SL + \gamma LV \cos \theta$$

2. Where:

a. γSV is the solid-vapor surface free energy,

b. γSL is the solid-liquid interfacial tension, and

c. γLV is the liquid-vapor surface tension.

3. Sessile Drop Method:

a. A droplet of liquid is placed on the solid surface, and its profile is analyzed. The contact angle provides information to calculate surface free energy.

4. Wilhelmy Plate Method:

a. A plate is immersed in a liquid, and the force on the plate is measured as it is pulled out. This method is used to determine the surface free energy of solids and liquids.

5. **Surface Tensiometry:**

   a. Techniques like drop weight, drop volume, and pendant drop methods are used to measure the surface tension of liquids, which can then be related to surface free energy.

Factors Affecting Surface Free Energy

1. **Surface Roughness and Heterogeneity:**

   a. Surface roughness increases the actual surface area and can either increase or decrease the apparent surface free energy depending on the nature of the roughness and the wetting liquid.

   b. Surface heterogeneity, including chemical composition variations, affects surface free energy by creating regions with different interaction energies.

2. **Surface Treatments and Coatings:**

   a. Treatments such as plasma cleaning, chemical etching, or coating with thin films can alter the surface chemistry and morphology, thereby modifying surface free energy.

3. **Environmental Factors:**

   a. Humidity, temperature, and exposure to different gases or liquids can change the surface state and thus its free energy.

Applications of Surface Free Energy

1. **Adhesion and Bonding:**

   a. Surface free energy is critical in adhesion processes. Materials with higher surface free energy typically show better adhesion because of stronger interfacial interactions.

   b. Adhesives are designed to match the surface free energy of substrates for optimal bonding.

2. **Coatings and Paints:**

   a. The spreadability and adhesion of coatings and paints depend on the surface free energy of both the coating material and the substrate.

Matching these energies ensures uniform coverage and strong adhesion.

3. **Wettability and Liquid Spreading:**
   a. The ability of a liquid to wet and spread on a surface is directly related to the surface free energy. Surfaces with high free energy are more easily wetted by liquids.
   b. Applications include inkjet printing, painting, and lubrication.

4. **Biomaterials and Medical Devices:**
   a. Surface free energy influences the interaction of biomaterials with biological tissues. For instance, surface modifications to enhance or reduce protein adsorption are tailored by adjusting surface free energy.

5. **Microfluidics and Lab-on-a-Chip Devices:**
   a. Controlling surface free energy is essential for directing fluid flow and ensuring proper functioning of microfluidic devices.

Advanced Concepts

1. **Young-Dupre Equation:**
   a. This equation relates the work of adhesion (W) to the surface free energies and the contact angle:

   $$W=\gamma L(1+\cos\theta)$$

   It provides insight into the energy required to separate a liquid droplet from a surface.

2. **Thermodynamic Considerations:**
   a. Surface free energy is a component of the Gibbs free energy change associated with creating new surfaces. It plays a role in processes like nucleation, crystallization, and phase separation.

3. **Surface Energy Anisotropy:**
   a. Crystalline materials can exhibit anisotropic surface free energies, meaning the energy varies with the crystallographic orientation of the

surface. This anisotropy affects phenomena like crystal growth and etching.

4. Dynamic Surface Free Energy:

    a. The surface free energy can change dynamically due to adsorption/desorption of molecules, surface reactions, or exposure to varying environmental conditions.

MEASUREMENT OF SURFACE TENSIONS

Accurate measurement of surface tension is crucial for understanding and manipulating surface and interfacial phenomena. Several methods are used to measure surface tension, each with its own principles, applications, and limitations.

1. Capillary Rise Method

Principle:

1. This method is based on the capillary action of a liquid rising or falling in a narrow tube. The height of the liquid column is used to calculate the surface tension.

Equation:

The surface tension γ can be calculated using Jurin's law:

$$\gamma = h\rho g r 2$$

Where:

h is the height of the liquid column, ρ is the density of the liquid, g is the acceleration due to gravity, and r is the radius of the capillary tube.

Procedure:

1. A capillary tube is partially immersed in the liquid.
2. The height h to which the liquid rises or falls is measured.
3. The radius r of the tube is also measured.
4. These values are plugged into the equation to calculate the surface tension.

Applications:

- Commonly used for clean liquids with low viscosity.
- Suitable for academic and research settings.

Limitations:

1. Accuracy depends on the precise measurement of the capillary tube radius and the liquid height.
2. Not suitable for highly viscous or non-Newtonian liquids.

2. Drop Weight and Drop Volume Methods

Principle:

1. These methods involve measuring the weight or volume of a droplet of liquid detaching from a nozzle or a capillary tube.

Equation:

The surface tension γ is calculated using:

$$\gamma = mg2\pi r$$

Where :

> m is the mass of the droplet, g is the acceleration due to gravity, and r is the radius of the nozzle.

Procedure:

1. A liquid is allowed to form droplets at the tip of a calibrated nozzle or capillary.
2. The mass or volume of the droplets is measured as they detach.
3. The radius of the nozzle is known or measured.
4. Surface tension is calculated using the mass or volume of the droplets and the radius of the nozzle.

Applications:

- Suitable for various liquids, including those with moderate viscosity.
- Often used in industrial settings and quality control.

Limitations:

1. Accuracy can be affected by evaporation, especially for volatile liquids.

2. Requires precise control and measurement of droplet formation.

3. Pendant Drop Method

Principle:

1. This method analyzes the shape of a liquid droplet suspended from a needle to determine surface tension based on the droplet profile.

Equation:

1. The Young-Laplace equation relates the shape of the droplet to the surface tension:

2. $\Delta P = \gamma(1R1 + 1R2)$

Where :

1. ΔP is the pressure difference across the interface, and $R1$ and $R2$ are the radii of curvature at different points on the droplet.

Procedure:

1. A droplet of liquid is suspended from the end of a needle.

2. The profile of the droplet is captured using a camera.

3. Image analysis software is used to fit the droplet shape and calculate the surface tension.

Applications:

1. Suitable for a wide range of liquids, including those with high viscosity.

2. Commonly used in research and industrial laboratories.

Limitations:

1. Requires sophisticated image analysis software.

2. Accuracy depends on the quality of the droplet profile image.

4. Wilhelmy Plate Method

Principle:

1. This method involves measuring the force exerted on a thin, vertically oriented plate partially immersed in a liquid.

Equation:

The surface tension γ is calculated using:

$$\gamma = FL$$

Where :

F is the force measured, and L is the perimeter of the plate in contact with the liquid.

Procedure:

1. A thin plate (often made of platinum or glass) is cleaned and partially immersed in the liquid.
2. The force exerted on the plate as it is pulled out of the liquid is measured using a sensitive balance.
3. The surface tension is calculated based on the measured force and the perimeter of the plate.

Applications:

1. Widely used for precise surface tension measurements in research and industrial quality control.
2. Suitable for various liquids, including those with low to moderate viscosity.

Limitations:

- Requires a clean, uniform plate surface.
- Sensitive to contamination and surface roughness.

5. Spinning Drop Method

Principle:

This method measures the interfacial tension by analyzing the shape of a drop of liquid inside another liquid in a rotating tube.

Equation:

The interfacial tension γ is calculated using:

$$\gamma = \Delta\rho\omega2R34$$

Where :

$\Delta\rho$ is the density difference between the two liquids, ω is the angular velocity, and R is the radius of the drop.

Procedure:

1. A small drop of one liquid is injected into another immiscible liquid inside a horizontal capillary tube.
2. The tube is rotated, and the drop elongates due to centrifugal forces.
3. The shape and dimensions of the drop are analyzed to calculate the interfacial tension.

Applications:

1. Suitable for measuring very low interfacial tensions.
2. Commonly used in the study of emulsions and microemulsions.

Limitations:

1. Requires specialized equipment and careful calibration.
2. Not suitable for high-viscosity liquids.

MEASUREMENT OF INTERFACIAL TENSIONS

Interfacial tension, the force per unit length existing at the interface between two immiscible phases (e.g., oil and water), is a critical parameter in many industrial and scientific applications. Various methods are employed to measure interfacial tension accurately, each with distinct principles and applications.

1. Pendant Drop Method

Principle:

1. This method involves analyzing the shape of a droplet of one liquid suspended in another immiscible liquid. The interfacial tension affects the droplet's profile.

Equation:

The Young-Laplace equation relates the pressure difference across the interface to the interfacial tension and the radii of curvature at different points on the droplet:

$$\Delta P = \left(\frac{1}{R_1} + \frac{1}{R_2}\right)$$

Where :

ΔP is the pressure difference, γ is the interfacial tension, and R_1 And R_2 are the radii of curvature.

Procedure:

1. A droplet of liquid A is suspended in liquid B using a needle.
2. The droplet's profile is captured using a high-resolution camera.
3. Image analysis software fits the droplet shape to theoretical models to calculate the interfacial tension.

Applications:

1. Suitable for a wide range of liquid pairs, including those with high viscosity differences.
2. Commonly used in research laboratories for precise measurements.

Limitations:

1. Requires sophisticated image analysis tools and software.
2. The accuracy depends on the quality of the droplet image and the precision of the shape fitting.

2. Spinning Drop Method

Principle:

1. This method measures interfacial tension by analyzing the shape of a drop of one liquid inside another immiscible liquid in a rotating tube. Centrifugal forces elongate the drop, and its shape is used to determine the interfacial tension.

Equation:

The interfacial tension γ is calculated using:

$$\gamma = \frac{\Delta \rho \, \omega^2 R^3}{4}$$

Where :

$\Delta\rho$ is the density difference between the two liquids, ω is the angular velocity, and R is the radius of the drop.

Procedure:

1. A small drop of liquid A is injected into liquid B inside a horizontal capillary tube.
2. The tube is rotated at a known angular velocity.
3. The shape and dimensions of the elongated drop are measured.
4. Interfacial tension is calculated using the drop's dimensions and the rotation speed.

Applications:

1. Ideal for measuring very low interfacial tensions, such as those found in emulsions and microemulsions.
2. Widely used in petrochemical and pharmaceutical industries.

Limitations:

1. Requires specialized equipment and precise control of rotation speed.
2. Not suitable for high-viscosity liquids.

3. Wilhelmy Plate Method

Principle:

1. This method measures the force exerted on a thin, vertically oriented plate partially immersed in a liquid-liquid interface. The force is related to the interfacial tension.

Equation:

The interfacial tension γ is calculated using:

$$\gamma = FL$$

Where :

F is the measured force, and L is the perimeter of the plate in contact with the interface.

Procedure:

1. A thin plate (often made of platinum or glass) is cleaned and partially immersed at the interface of two immiscible liquids.
2. The force exerted on the plate is measured as it is pulled through the interface using a sensitive balance.
3. The interfacial tension is calculated based on the measured force and the perimeter of the plate.

Applications:

- Suitable for a wide range of liquid pairs.
- Commonly used in research and industrial quality control.

Limitations:

1. Requires a clean, uniform plate surface to ensure accuracy.
2. Sensitive to surface contamination and roughness.

4. Drop Weight and Drop Volume Methods

Principle:

These methods involve measuring the weight or volume of a droplet of one liquid detaching from a nozzle or a capillary tube into another immiscible liquid.

Equation:

The interfacial tension γ can be determined using the weight or volume of the droplet and the radius of the nozzle or capillary.

Procedure:

1. Liquid A is allowed to form droplets at the tip of a nozzle or capillary submerged in liquid B.
2. The mass or volume of the droplets is measured as they detach.
3. The radius of the nozzle or capillary is known or measured.
4. Interfacial tension is calculated using the mass or volume of the droplets and the nozzle or capillary radius.

Applications:

1. Suitable for various liquid pairs, including those with moderate viscosity differences.

2. Often used in industrial settings and quality control laboratories.

Limitations:

1. Accuracy can be affected by evaporation, especially for volatile liquids.

2. Requires precise control and measurement of droplet formation.

5. Sessile Drop Method

Principle:

This method involves placing a droplet of one liquid on a solid substrate in the presence of another immiscible liquid. The shape and contact angle of the droplet are analyzed to determine interfacial tension.

Equation:

Interfacial tension is inferred from the contact angle and the shape of the droplet using theoretical models and numerical calculations.

Procedure:

- A droplet of liquid A is placed on a solid substrate submerged in liquid B.

- The droplet's profile and contact angle are captured using a high-resolution camera.

- Image analysis software fits the droplet shape to models to calculate the interfacial tension.

Applications:

1. Suitable for studying solid-liquid-liquid interfaces.

2. Commonly used in surface science and materials research.

Limitations:

1. Requires accurate image capture and sophisticated analysis software.

2. Sensitive to the cleanliness and uniformity of the solid substrate.

SPREADING COEFFICIENT

The spreading coefficient is an important concept in surface and interfacial phenomena, describing the ability of one liquid to spread over another. It is crucial in applications like coating, emulsification, and detergency.

Definition and Concept

1. **Spreading Coefficient (S):**
   a. The spreading coefficient, S, quantifies the tendency of a liquid to spread spontaneously over another liquid or solid surface.
   b. It is defined as the difference between the work of adhesion (W_a) and the work of cohesion (W_c) of the spreading liquid.

Equation:

$$S = \gamma SV - (\gamma SL + \gamma LV)$$

where:

γSV is the surface tension of the solid in the vapor.

γSL is the interfacial tension between the solid and the liquid.

γLV is the surface tension of the liquid in the vapor.

Physical Interpretation

1. **Positive Spreading Coefficient:**
   a. If $S>0$, the liquid will spontaneously spread over the surface, forming a thin, continuous film.
   b. This indicates that the adhesive forces between the liquid and the surface are greater than the cohesive forces within the liquid.

2. **Negative Spreading Coefficient:**
   a. If $S<0$, the liquid will not spread spontaneously and instead will form droplets or a non-uniform layer.
   b. This indicates that the cohesive forces within the liquid are greater than the adhesive forces between the liquid and the surface.

Measurement of Spreading Coefficient

1. **Contact Angle Method:**
   a. The spreading coefficient can be indirectly measured using the contact angle of a liquid on a solid surface.

b. A lower contact angle suggests better spreading, correlating with a higher spreading coefficient.

Equation:

Where : θ is the contact angle of the liquid on the surface.

2.   Direct Measurement:

Direct measurement involves observing the behavior of a droplet of liquid on the surface of another liquid or solid and calculating the spreading coefficient based on observed spreading or contraction.

Factors Affecting Spreading Coefficient

1. Surface Tensions:

The intrinsic surface tensions (γSV,, and γLV) directly influence the spreading coefficient. Lower interfacial tension between the liquid and the surface favors spreading.

2. Temperature:

Temperature affects surface and interfacial tensions. Generally, an increase in temperature decreases surface tension, potentially increasing the spreading coefficient.

3. Surface Roughness and Heterogeneity:

Surface roughness and heterogeneity can either enhance or hinder spreading, depending on the nature of the liquid and the surface.

4. Presence of Surfactants:

Surfactants can significantly alter the surface and interfacial tensions, often enhancing spreading by reducing γLV and γSL.

Applications of Spreading Coefficient

1. Coating and Painting:

A high spreading coefficient ensures uniform coverage of coatings and paints, leading to better surface finish and protection.

2. Emulsification:

In emulsions, the spreading coefficient influences the stability and distribution of droplets, crucial in food, pharmaceutical, and cosmetic industries.

3. **Detergency:**

Effective spreading of detergents over oily or dirty surfaces enhances cleaning efficiency.

4. **Inkjet Printing:**

The spreading coefficient affects ink behavior on substrates, impacting print quality and resolution.

5. **Biomedical Applications:**

Spreading properties are important in drug delivery systems, where uniform distribution of bioactive liquids over tissues or materials is needed.

Advanced Concepts

1. **Young-Dupre Equation:**

   a. Relates the contact angle to the work of adhesion, providing a theoretical framework to understand spreading phenomena.

$$Wa=\gamma L(1+\cos\theta)$$

2. **Thermodynamic Considerations:**

   a. Spreading is a thermodynamic process driven by minimizing the system's free energy. The spreading coefficient provides insight into the energetics of this process.

3. **Dynamic Spreading:**

   a. In real-world applications, spreading is often a dynamic process influenced by time-dependent factors like evaporation, adsorption, and viscoelastic properties of the liquids involved.

Adsorption At Liquid Interfaces

Adsorption at liquid interfaces is a critical aspect of surface and interfacial phenomena. It involves the accumulation of molecules at the interface between two immiscible liquids (e.g., oil and water) or between a liquid and a gas (e.g., water and air). This process significantly impacts various industrial and biological processes, such as emulsification, detergency, and drug delivery.

Definition and Concept

Adsorption:

1. Adsorption is the process where molecules from a bulk phase accumulate at an interface, forming a distinct layer.
2. It differs from absorption, where molecules uniformly penetrate into the bulk of a phase.

Liquid Interface:

1. The interface between two immiscible liquids (liquid-liquid interface) or between a liquid and a gas (liquid-gas interface).

Surface Excess:

The amount of a substance adsorbed at the interface, often described by the surface excess concentration, Γ.

Gibbs Adsorption Isotherm:

Relates the change in surface tension to the surface excess of the adsorbed species.

$$d\gamma d \ln[\text{\textit{fo}}]C = -RT\Gamma$$

Where :

γ is the surface tension, C is the concentration of the adsorbate, R is the gas constant, and T is the temperature.

Mechanisms of Adsorption

1. Physical Adsorption (Physisorption):

  a. Involves weak van der Waals forces.
  b. Reversible and typically occurs at lower temperatures.
  c. Example: Adsorption of gases on water surfaces.

2. Chemical Adsorption (Chemisorption):

a. Involves stronger chemical bonds, such as covalent or ionic bonds.

b. Often irreversible and occurs at higher temperatures.

c. Example: Adsorption of surfactants at oil-water interfaces.

Factors Affecting Adsorption

1. Nature of Adsorbate:

a. Molecular size, polarity, and functional groups influence adsorption.

b. Surfactants and amphiphilic molecules tend to adsorb readily due to their dual affinity for both phases.

2. Concentration of Adsorbate:

a. Higher concentrations generally increase adsorption until saturation is reached.

3. Temperature:

a. Higher temperatures can either enhance or reduce adsorption depending on the nature of the adsorption process (exothermic or endothermic).

4. pH and Ionic Strength:

a. pH affects the ionization state of the adsorbate and the interface, influencing adsorption.

b. Ionic strength can impact electrostatic interactions, affecting adsorption behavior.

5. Presence of Other Substances:

a. Competing species can inhibit or enhance adsorption through competitive adsorption or synergistic effects.

Measurement of Adsorption

1. Surface Tension Measurement:

a. Changes in surface or interfacial tension upon adsorption can be measured using tensiometry methods like the Wilhelmy plate, pendant drop, or drop volume methods.

b. The Gibbs adsorption isotherm can be applied to relate surface tension changes to surface excess concentration.

2. **Ellipsometry:**

   a. An optical technique that measures the change in polarization of light reflected from the interface, providing information on the thickness and refractive index of the adsorbed layer.

3. **Quartz Crystal Microbalance (QCM):**

   a. Measures the change in frequency of a quartz crystal resonator, which is proportional to the mass of the adsorbed layer.

4. **Surface Plasmon Resonance (SPR):**

   a. **Monitors changes in the refractive index near the interface, providing real**-time data on adsorption kinetics and equilibrium.

5. **Neutron and X-ray Reflectometry:**

   a. Provides detailed information on the structure and composition of adsorbed layers at interfaces.

Applications of Adsorption at Liquid Interfaces

1. **Emulsions and Foams:**

   a. Surfactants adsorb at oil-water or air-water interfaces, stabilizing emulsions and foams by reducing interfacial tension and forming protective layers.

2. **Detergency and Cleaning:**

   a. Adsorption of surfactants at interfaces enhances the removal of oils and dirt from surfaces by reducing interfacial tension and improving wetting.

3. **Drug Delivery:**

   a. Adsorption of drugs at interfaces can enhance bioavailability and targeted delivery by controlling the interaction between drugs and biological membranes.

4. **Food and Cosmetic Products:**

a. Stabilization of emulsions in food products and creams is achieved through the adsorption of emulsifiers at oil-water interfaces.

5. Corrosion Inhibition:

a. Adsorption of inhibitors at metal-liquid interfaces can protect against corrosion by forming a protective barrier.

Theoretical Models of Adsorption

1. Langmuir Adsorption Isotherm:

Assumes monolayer adsorption on a homogeneous surface with a finite number of identical sites.

$$\Gamma = \Gamma max KC 1 + KC$$

Where :

1. Γmax is the maximum adsorption capacity, K is the adsorption equilibrium constant, and C is the adsorbate concentration.

2. Freundlich Adsorption Isotherm:

a. Describes adsorption on heterogeneous surfaces with varying affinities.

$$\Gamma = Kf C 1/n$$

Where :

Kf and n are empirical constants.

3. Gibbs Adsorption Equation:

a. Relates changes in surface tension to surface excess concentration, providing a thermodynamic basis for adsorption at interfaces.

SURFACE ACTIVE AGENTS

Surface active agents, commonly known as surfactants, are compounds that preferentially adsorb at the interface between two phases (e.g., liquid-gas, liquid-liquid, or liquid-solid) and significantly alter the properties of the interface. These molecules contain both hydrophilic (water-attracting) and hydrophobic (water-repelling) parts, which give them their unique interfacial activity.

Structure of Surfactants

Surfactants typically consist of two distinct regions:

1. **Hydrophilic Head**: This part of the molecule is polar or ionic and is attracted to water. It can be charged (anionic, cationic) or neutral (nonionic).

2. **Hydrophobic Tail**: This part is nonpolar and repels water. It is usually a long hydrocarbon chain that interacts preferentially with oils and other nonpolar substances.

Classification of Surfactants

Surfactants are classified based on the nature of their hydrophilic head:

1. Anionic Surfactants:

   a. Contain a negatively charged head group.

   b. **Common examples:** Sodium dodecyl sulfate (SDS), soap (fatty acid salts).

   c. **Applications:** Detergents, shampoos, foaming agents.

2. Cationic Surfactants:

   a. Contain a positively charged head group.

   b. **Common examples**: Cetyltrimethylammonium bromide (CTAB), benzalkonium chloride.

   c. **Applications:** Fabric softeners, disinfectants, hair conditioners.

3. Nonionic Surfactants:

   a. Contain a neutral, polar head group, often consisting of ethylene oxide chains.

   b. **Common examples:** Polyethylene glycol (PEG), Tween, Span.

c. **Application**s: Emulsifiers, wetting agents, dispersants.

4. **Amphoteric (Zwitterionic) Surfactants:**

    a. Contain both positive and negative charges within the same molecule.

    b. **Common examples**: Cocamidopropyl betaine.

    c. **Applications**: Mild shampoos, body washes, personal care products.

Mechanisms of Action

Surfactants reduce the surface or interfacial tension by adsorbing at the interface, leading to several important effects:

1. **Reduction of Surface Tension:**

    a. Surfactants lower the surface tension of water, enhancing wetting and spreading properties.

2. **Formation of Micelles:**

    a. Above a certain concentration, known as the critical micelle concentration (CMC), surfactants form micelles. In micelles, the hydrophobic tails are sequestered away from water, while the hydrophilic heads face the aqueous environment.

    b. Micelles play a crucial role in solubilizing hydrophobic substances in water.

3. **Stabilization of Emulsions and Foams:**

    a. By reducing interfacial tension, surfactants help stabilize emulsions (mixtures of oil and water) and foams (gas bubbles in a liquid).

4. **Detergency and Cleaning:**

    a. Surfactants aid in removing dirt and oils from surfaces by emulsifying oily substances and suspending them in water.

Applications of Surfactants

1. **Detergents and Cleaning Agents:**

    a. Surfactants are the primary active ingredients in household and industrial cleaning products. They enhance the removal of dirt, grease, and stains by emulsifying oils and wetting surfaces.

2. **Emulsification in Food and Cosmetics:**
   a. Surfactants stabilize emulsions in food products (e.g., mayonnaise, salad dressings) and cosmetic formulations (e.g., lotions, creams).

3. **Pharmaceuticals and Drug Delivery:**
   a. Surfactants are used to enhance the solubility and bioavailability of drugs, stabilize emulsions, and form drug delivery systems like liposomes and microemulsions.

4. **Enhanced Oil Recovery (EOR):**
   a. In the petroleum industry, surfactants are used to lower the interfacial tension between oil and water, improving the extraction of oil from reservoirs.

5. **Agricultural Products:**
   a. Surfactants are used in pesticides and herbicides to enhance wetting, spreading, and penetration of active ingredients on plant surfaces.

6. **Personal Care Products:**
   a. Shampoos, conditioners, body washes, and toothpastes contain surfactants for their foaming, emulsifying, and cleaning properties.

Environmental and Health Considerations

1. **Biodegradability:**
   a. The environmental impact of surfactants is a significant concern. Biodegradable surfactants are preferred to reduce environmental pollution.

2. **Toxicity:**
   a. The toxicity of surfactants to aquatic life and human health is evaluated to ensure safety. Nonionic and amphoteric surfactants are generally less irritating than anionic and cationic surfactants.

3. **Regulations:**

a. Various regulations govern the use of surfactants in different industries to ensure they meet safety and environmental standards.

HLB SCALE

he Hydrophilic-Lipophilic Balance (HLB) scale is a crucial concept in the field of surface and interfacial phenomena, particularly in the formulation of emulsions and surfactant-based products. Developed by William C. Griffin in the 1940s, the HLB scale is a numerical system used to characterize the balance between the hydrophilic (water-attracting) and lipophilic (oil-attracting) properties of surfactants.

Definition and Concept

1. Hydrophilic-Lipophilic Balance (HLB):

    a. The HLB value of a surfactant quantifies its ability to form stable emulsions by determining its affinity for the oil and water phases.

    b. It is a scale ranging typically from 1 to 20, where higher values indicate greater hydrophilicity and lower values indicate greater lipophilicity.

Calculation of HLB Value

1. Griffin's Method:

    a. The original method developed by Griffin involves assigning specific weightings to different functional groups within the surfactant molecule.

    b. The HLB value is calculated based on the weighted sum of these groups.

2. Davies' Method:

    a. An alternative method proposed by Davies simplifies the calculation by considering the relative proportions of hydrophilic and lipophilic groups in the surfactant molecule.

Application of HLB in Emulsion Formulation

1. **Oil-in-Water (O/W) Emulsions:**

    a. Surfactants with higher HLB values (typically above 10) are more hydrophilic and suitable for stabilizing oil-in-water emulsions.

    b. These surfactants promote the dispersion of oil droplets in the continuous aqueous phase.

2. **Water-in-Oil (W/O) Emulsions:**

    a. Surfactants with lower HLB values (typically below 10) are more lipophilic and are preferred for stabilizing water-in-oil emulsions.

    b. These surfactants promote the dispersion of water droplets in the continuous oil phase.

Selection of Surfactants Based on HLB

1. **HLB Matching:**

    a. Formulators select surfactants with HLB values that match the desired type of emulsion.

    b. The HLB values of individual surfactants can be adjusted by blending different types of surfactants or by modifying their molecular structure.

2. **HLB Testing:**

    a. Various experimental methods, including titration and phase inversion techniques, are used to determine the HLB value of surfactant blends and formulations.

Importance of HLB in Product Development

1. **Optimization of Emulsion Stability:**

    a. Proper selection and balance of surfactants based on HLB values are critical for achieving and maintaining emulsion stability.

    b. Incorrect HLB values can lead to phase separation, creaming, or coalescence of emulsion droplets.

2. **Formulation Flexibility:**

a. Understanding the HLB concept allows formulators to tailor emulsions and other surfactant-based products to specific requirements, such as viscosity, texture, and sensory attributes.

3. **Efficiency and Cost-Effectiveness:**

   a. Optimizing HLB values minimizes the amount of surfactant required to stabilize emulsions, leading to more cost-effective formulations.

Limitations and Considerations

1. **Simplification of Molecular Complexity:**

   a. The HLB scale provides a simplified characterization of surfactant properties and may not fully capture the complex interactions between surfactant molecules and interfaces.

2. **Temperature and pH Effects:**

   a. The HLB value of a surfactant may vary with temperature, pH, and other environmental factors, impacting its performance in different formulations.

3. **Specificity to Emulsions:**

   a. While the HLB scale is primarily used for emulsion formulation, its principles can also be applied to other surfactant-based systems, such as detergents and foaming agents.

SOLUBILIZATION

Solubilization refers to the process by which one substance, called the solute, is uniformly dispersed and stabilized within another substance, called the solvent, to form a homogeneous solution. In the context of surface and interfacial phenomena, solubilization often involves the dispersion of hydrophobic substances in aqueous solutions with the aid of surfactants or other amphiphilic molecules. This process is crucial in various industrial, pharmaceutical, and biological applications.

Mechanism of Solubilization

1. **Micelle Formation:**

a. Surfactants, which contain both hydrophilic and hydrophobic regions, self-assemble into micelles in solution.

b. In the presence of hydrophobic solutes, such as oils or nonpolar molecules, the hydrophobic tails of surfactants associate with the solutes, while the hydrophilic heads remain in contact with the aqueous phase.

c. This arrangement stabilizes the solubilized molecules within the hydrophobic core of the micelle, effectively increasing their solubility in the aqueous medium.

2. Microemulsions:

a. Microemulsions are thermodynamically stable, optically clear dispersions of oil droplets in water, stabilized by surfactants and sometimes cosurfactants.

b. Unlike conventional emulsions, microemulsions are transparent and have low interfacial tension, allowing for efficient solubilization of both hydrophobic and hydrophilic substances.

c. Microemulsions are formed through the spontaneous organization of surfactant molecules into structures known as micelles, which encapsulate the solubilized substances within their cores.

Factors Affecting Solubilization

1. Surfactant Structure and Concentration:

a. The molecular structure of surfactants, including the length and flexibility of hydrophobic tails and the charge and size of hydrophilic heads, influences their solubilizing capacity.

b. Increasing surfactant concentration generally enhances solubilization by promoting micelle formation and increasing the available hydrophobic core.

2. Nature of Solubilizate:

a. The chemical structure, size, and hydrophobicity of the solubilizate molecules affect their solubility and tendency to be encapsulated within micelles or microemulsions.

b. Highly hydrophobic molecules are more efficiently solubilized, while hydrophilic molecules may require specific surfactant structures or conditions for solubilization.

3. Temperature and pH:

a. Temperature and pH can influence the solubility of both surfactants and solubilizates, affecting the formation and stability of micelles and microemulsions.

b. Changes in temperature may also alter the phase behavior and solubilizing capacity of the system.

4. Cosurfactants and Additives:

a. Cosurfactants, such as alcohols or glycols, can enhance solubilization by modifying the interfacial properties of surfactant micelles and increasing their flexibility.

b. Additives, such as electrolytes or polymers, may also impact solubilization by affecting the structure and stability of micelles and microemulsions.

Applications of Solubilization

1. Pharmaceuticals:

a. Solubilization enables the formulation of poorly water-soluble drugs into oral, topical, and injectable dosage forms, enhancing their bioavailability and therapeutic efficacy.

b. Solubilized drug formulations may include micellar solutions, microemulsions, or lipid-based delivery systems.

2. Cosmetics and Personal Care Products:

a. Solubilization facilitates the incorporation of hydrophobic ingredients, such as fragrances, vitamins, and oils, into cosmetic formulations, improving their stability and sensory properties.

b. Micellar solutions and microemulsions are commonly used as delivery systems for active ingredients in skincare and haircare products.

3. **Food and Beverage Industry:**

a. Solubilization plays a crucial role in the formulation of food additives, flavors, and nutraceuticals, allowing for their uniform dispersion in aqueous matrices and enhancing their functionality.

b. Microemulsions and emulsifiers are used to improve the solubility and stability of oil-soluble vitamins, colors, and flavors in food and beverage products.

4. **Agrochemicals:**

a. Solubilization assists in the formulation of pesticides, herbicides, and fertilizers, enabling their dispersion and absorption in aqueous solutions for efficient application and uptake by plants.

5. **Enhanced Oil Recovery (EOR):**

a. Solubilization techniques, such as the use of surfactant floods or microemulsions, are employed to solubilize and mobilize trapped oil in reservoirs, increasing oil recovery from mature oil fields.

Challenges and Considerations

1. **Surfactant Toxicity and Biocompatibility:**

a. The selection of surfactants for solubilization applications requires consideration of their toxicity, biodegradability, and compatibility with the intended use, particularly in pharmaceutical and personal care formulations.

2. **Physical Stability and Shelf Life:**

a. Ensuring the physical stability and long-term shelf life of solubilized formulations, such as micellar solutions and microemulsions, may require optimization of surfactant composition, formulation conditions, and packaging.

3. Regulatory Requirements:

a. Regulatory requirements and guidelines must be followed in the development and commercialization of solubilized products, especially in industries such as pharmaceuticals and food, to ensure safety and compliance with applicable regulations.

DETERGENCY

Detergency refers to the ability of cleaning agents, such as detergents, to remove dirt, oils, grease, and other contaminants from surfaces through a combination of physical and chemical mechanisms. It is a fundamental aspect of surface and interfacial phenomena, with widespread applications in household cleaning, industrial processes, personal care products, and more. Understanding the principles of detergency involves knowledge of surfactants, emulsification, wetting, and other interfacial phenomena.

Mechanisms of Detergency

1. Wetting:

a. Detergents reduce the surface tension of water, allowing it to spread more easily over surfaces and penetrate into crevices and pores, facilitating the loosening and removal of dirt and contaminants.

2. Emulsification:

a. Detergents solubilize and emulsify oils and grease by forming micelles around hydrophobic molecules. These micelles suspend the oil droplets in water, preventing them from re-depositing onto surfaces.

3. Dispersing and Solubilizing:

a. Detergents break down and disperse insoluble particles, such as dirt and stains, into smaller fragments or colloidal suspensions, which can then be washed away with water.

b. Surfactants enhance the solubility of hydrophobic substances in water by forming stable micelles or microemulsions, effectively removing them from surfaces.

4. Chemical Reactions:

a. Some detergents contain enzymes or other chemical agents that break down specific types of stains or contaminants through chemical reactions, such as hydrolysis or oxidation.

Components of Detergents

1. Surfactants:

a. Surfactants are the primary active ingredients in detergents, responsible for reducing surface tension, emulsifying oils, and enhancing wetting and dispersion.

b. Anionic, cationic, nonionic, or amphoteric surfactants may be used depending on the type of soil and the cleaning conditions.

2. Builders:

a. Builders are additives that enhance the cleaning efficiency of detergents by sequestering hard water ions (e.g., calcium and magnesium) and preventing them from interfering with surfactant action.

b. Common builders include phosphates, zeolites, citrates, and polyphosphates.

3. Chelating Agents:

a. Chelating agents bind metal ions, such as iron and manganese, which can cause discoloration or contribute to the degradation of detergents and fabrics.

4. Enzymes:

a. Enzymes are biological catalysts that break down specific types of stains, such as protein-based stains (e.g., blood) or carbohydrate-based stains (e.g., food residues), into smaller, water-soluble fragments.

5. Optical Brighteners:

  a. Optical brighteners are fluorescent compounds that absorb ultraviolet light and emit visible blue light, making fabrics appear brighter and whiter.

Factors Affecting Detergency

1. Surfactant Concentration:

  a. Increasing the concentration of surfactants generally improves detergency by enhancing wetting, emulsification, and soil removal.

2. Water Hardness:

  a. Hard water, which contains high concentrations of calcium and magnesium ions, can reduce the effectiveness of detergents by forming insoluble precipitates with surfactants.

  b. Builders and chelating agents help mitigate the effects of hard water by sequestering these ions.

3. Temperature:

  a. Elevated temperatures can enhance the cleaning efficiency of detergents by accelerating chemical reactions, increasing solubility, and reducing the viscosity of soil.

4. pH:

  a. The pH of the cleaning solution can influence the solubility of soils and the stability of surfactants. Neutral or slightly alkaline pH is often preferred for general-purpose detergents.

5. Soil Type and Composition:

  a. Different types of soils, such as greasy stains, proteinaceous stains, or mineral deposits, may require specific detergent formulations or cleaning techniques for effective removal.

Applications of Detergency

1. Household Cleaning:

a. Detergents are used for cleaning floors, surfaces, dishes, laundry, and other household items, removing dirt, stains, and odors effectively.

2. **Industrial Cleaning:**

   a. In industrial settings, detergents are employed for cleaning equipment, machinery, vehicles, and manufacturing facilities, maintaining cleanliness and hygiene standards.

3. **Personal Care Products:**

   a. Detergent-based formulations, such as shampoos, body washes, and hand soaps, cleanse the skin and hair by removing oils, dirt, and impurities.

4. **Textile and Fabric Care:**

   a. Laundry detergents and fabric softeners clean and condition fabrics, removing stains, odors, and wrinkles while preserving color and texture.

5. **Food and Beverage Processing:**

   a. Detergents are used for cleaning and sanitizing equipment and surfaces in food processing plants, breweries, and restaurants, ensuring food safety and quality.

Environmental and Health Considerations

1. **Biodegradability:**

   a. Biodegradable detergents break down into non-toxic substances, reducing environmental impact and promoting sustainability.

2. **Low Phosphate and Low VOC Formulations:**

   a. Phosphates, volatile organic compounds (VOCs), and other harmful chemicals are minimized or eliminated in eco-friendly detergents to protect ecosystems and human health.

3. **Safety and Irritation:**

a. Detergents should be formulated to be safe for users and non-irritating to skin and mucous membranes, especially in personal care products and cleaning agents used in sensitive environments.

ADSORPTION AT SOLID INTERFACE

Adsorption at solid interfaces is a fundamental phenomenon in surface science and plays a crucial role in various industrial processes, including catalysis, chromatography, and material synthesis. Understanding the mechanisms and factors influencing adsorption at solid surfaces is essential for optimizing processes and designing advanced materials with tailored properties.

Definition and Concept

1. Adsorption:

    a. Adsorption is the accumulation of molecules or atoms at the surface of a solid material due to attractive forces between the adsorbate (molecules or atoms) and the solid surface.

    b. Adsorption can occur through physical interactions (physisorption) or chemical reactions (chemisorption) between the adsorbate and the surface.

2. Solid Interface:

    a. The interface between a solid material and a gas or liquid phase where adsorption occurs.

    b. Solid interfaces can be characterized by their surface properties, such as roughness, morphology, and chemical composition.

Mechanisms of Adsorption

1. Physisorption:

    a. Physisorption involves weak van der Waals interactions between the adsorbate and the solid surface.

    b. It is typically reversible and depends on factors such as surface area, temperature, and the nature of the adsorbate and adsorbent.

2. Chemisorption:

a. Chemisorption involves stronger chemical bonds, such as covalent or ionic bonds, between the adsorbate and the solid surface.

b. It is often irreversible and may involve electron transfer or chemical reactions at the interface.

Factors Affecting Adsorption

1. **Surface Properties:**

   a. Surface area, roughness, morphology, and chemical composition of the solid interface influence the adsorption capacity and affinity for different adsorbates.

2. **Nature of Adsorbate:**

   a. The chemical structure, polarity, size, and concentration of the adsorbate affect its interaction with the solid surface and the extent of adsorption.

3. **Temperature:**

   a. Temperature influences the adsorption equilibrium by affecting the energy of adsorption and desorption processes.

4. **Pressure:**

   a. Pressure can affect adsorption behavior, particularly at high pressures where gas molecules may undergo condensation or multilayer adsorption.

5. **pH and Ionic Strength:**

   a. pH and ionic strength of the solution can influence surface charge and electrostatic interactions, affecting adsorption of charged species.

Techniques for Studying Adsorption

1. **Surface Analysis Techniques:**

   a. Techniques such as X-ray photoelectron spectroscopy (XPS), scanning electron microscopy (SEM), and atomic force microscopy (AFM) provide information about surface composition, morphology, and topography.

2. **Adsorption Isotherms:**
   a. Adsorption isotherms measure the relationship between the adsorbate concentration in the bulk phase and the amount adsorbed onto the solid surface at equilibrium.
   b. Common isotherm models include the Langmuir, Freundlich, and BET **(Brunauer-Emmett-Teller) isotherms.**

3. **Surface Area and Porosity Analysis:**
   a. Techniques such as nitrogen adsorption-desorption isotherms and mercury intrusion porosimetry measure surface area, pore volume, and pore size distribution of porous materials.

4. **Dynamic Adsorption Studies:**
   a. Dynamic adsorption studies involve monitoring adsorption kinetics and the rate of adsorbate uptake onto the solid surface over time.

Applications of Adsorption at Solid Interfaces

1. **Catalysis:**
   a. Solid catalysts facilitate chemical reactions by adsorbing reactant molecules onto their surface, providing active sites for reaction pathways.

2. **Gas Separation and Purification:**
   a. Adsorbent materials such as activated carbon and zeolites selectively adsorb gases based on their molecular size, polarity, and affinity for the solid surface.

3. **Chromatography:**
   a. Solid phases in chromatographic columns selectively adsorb analytes from a mobile phase based on their interactions with the stationary phase, allowing for separation and analysis of complex mixtures.

4. **Environmental Remediation:**

a. Adsorbent materials are used to remove pollutants and contaminants from air and water through processes such as adsorption, ion exchange, and filtration.

5. Surface Modification and Functionalization:

a. Adsorption techniques are employed to modify and functionalize solid surfaces with desired properties, such as increased hydrophobicity, catalytic activity, or bioaffinity.

Challenges and Future Directions

1. Understanding Surface-Adsorbate Interactions:

a. Elucidating the complex interactions between adsorbates and solid surfaces at the molecular level remains a challenge, requiring advanced theoretical and experimental techniques.

2. Tailoring Surface Properties:

a. Designing materials with tailored surface properties for specific adsorption applications requires precise control over surface composition, morphology, and reactivity.

3. Environmental and Sustainability Considerations:

a. Developing environmentally friendly adsorbent materials and processes that minimize energy consumption, waste generation, and environmental impact is a growing priority.

Multiple choice questions (MCQs) :

1. What is surface tension primarily a result of?

   A) Adhesion between molecules.

   B) Cohesion between molecules.

   C) Gravity acting on molecules.

   D) Electrical charges among molecules.

2. Which phenomenon describes the ability of a liquid to flow in narrow spaces without the assistance of external forces?

    A) Adsorption

    B) Wettability

    C) Capillarity

    D) Surfactancy

3. What is the typical unit for measuring surface tension?

    A) Pascal

    B) Newton per meter

    C) Joules

    D) Meters per second squared

4. Which method is NOT a method of measuring surface tension?

    A) Capillary Rise Method

    B) Pendant Drop Method

    C) Tensiometer Method

    D) Boiling Point Elevation Method

5. Which type of adsorption involves the formation of chemical bonds?

    A) Physisorption

    B) Chemisorption

    C) Capillary condensation

    D) Sieving

6. Which surfactant type has a hydrophilic head and a hydrophobic tail?

    A) Enzymes

    B) Catalysts

    C) Surfactants

    D) Solvents

7. What does the contact angle of a liquid on a solid surface primarily measure?

    A) Viscosity of the liquid

    B) Temperature of the liquid

C) Wettability of the surface

D) Elasticity of the surface

8. What effect does temperature generally have on surface tension?

A) Increases as temperature increases

B) Decreases as temperature increases

C) Does not change with temperature

D) Increases then decreases with temperature

9. Which phenomenon is correctly paired with its description?

A) Capillarity - Mixing of two immiscible liquids

B) Marangoni Effect - Mass transfer due to tension gradients

C) Adsorption - Increase in kinetic energy at interfaces

D) Detergency - Reduction of intermolecular forces at interfaces

10. What is the main purpose of surfactants in detergents?

A) Increase water viscosity

B) Decrease water boiling point

C) Reduce surface tension

D) Increase pH levels

11. Which is NOT a typical application of surface tension knowledge?

A) Predicting weather patterns

B) Formulating detergents

C) Developing emulsions

D) Enhancing coating processes

12. Which method involves the use of a rotating tube to measure interfacial tension?

A) Pendant Drop Method

B) Spinning Drop Method

C) Sessile Drop Method

D) Wilhelmy Plate Method

13. What is the primary effect of adding surfactants to water in cleaning processes?

   A) Increasing water hardness

   B) Reducing interfacial tension

   C) Decreasing water density

   D) Elevating water temperature

14. Which method analyzes the shape of a droplet to measure surface tension?

   A) Tensiometer Method

   B) Pendant Drop Method

   C) Sessile Drop Method

   D) Spinning Drop Method

15. What is primarily assessed by the Wilhelmy Plate Method?

   A) Viscosity of liquids

   B) Boiling point of liquids

   C) Surface tension of liquids

   D) Thermal conductivity of liquids

16. Which of the following statements is true about surfactants?

   A) They increase the boiling point of liquids.

   B) They are only used in pharmaceutical applications.

   C) They stabilize emulsions by reducing interfacial tension.

   D) They increase the viscosity of liquids.

17. Which factor does NOT influence the measurement of surface tension?

   A) Temperature of the liquid

   B) Purity of the liquid

   C) Color of the liquid

   D) Presence of impurities in the liquid

18. Which type of adsorption is generally reversible?

   A) Chemisorption

   B) Physisorption

C) Capillary action

D) Thermal expansion

19. What role do enzymes play in detergents?

A) They stabilize the detergent structure.

B) They break down specific types of stains.

C) They increase the boiling point of detergents.

D) They reduce the detergent's surface tension.

20. Which factor is crucial for the design of surfactants used in emulsions?

A) Hydrophilic-Lipophilic Balance (HLB)

B) Thermal stability

C) Electrical conductivity

D) Magnetic properties

Short Answer Type Questions

1. What is surface tension and how is it measured?

2. Explain the concept of interfacial tension and its significance in emulsions.

3. What is adsorption? Distinguish between physisorption and chemisorption.

4. Describe the role of surfactants in reducing surface and interfacial tension.

5. What factors influence the wettability of a surface by a liquid?

6. How does temperature affect surface tension?

7. Define capillarity and give an example of its application.

8. What is the Marangoni effect and where is it commonly observed?

9. Explain how detergents use surfactants to remove oils and dirt from surfaces.

10. What are the applications of surface and interfacial phenomena in biological systems?

11. Discuss the impact of surface roughness on surface free energy.

12. How do contact angles measure the wettability of a surface?

13. What is the Wilhelmy Plate Method used for?

14. Explain the role of enzymes in detergents.

15. Describe the Young-Laplace equation and its importance in surface phenomena.

16. What is the significance of the critical micelle concentration (CMC) in surfactant solutions?

17. Explain the Gibbs adsorption isotherm and its relevance in surface chemistry.

18. What are micelles and how do they contribute to the function of detergents?

19. How do surfactants stabilize emulsions?

20. Define the spreading coefficient and discuss its implications in coatings.

Long Answer Type Questions

1. Discuss the various methods used to measure surface tension and the principles behind each method.

2. Explain the role of surface active agents (surfactants) in various industries and how they modify interfacial properties.

3. Describe the factors that affect the performance of surfactants in emulsification and detergency processes.

4. Analyze the impact of surface and interfacial phenomena on the formulation and stability of pharmaceuticals.

5. Provide a detailed explanation of how adsorption at liquid interfaces is critical for processes like detergency and drug delivery.

6. Explore the relationship between surface free energy, adhesion, and wettability in materials science applications.

7. Discuss the use of the Young-Laplace equation in describing the behavior of liquid droplets and the formation of bubbles.

8. Elaborate on the mechanisms by which surfactants aid in enhanced oil recovery (EOR) and their environmental considerations.

9. Detail the role and mechanisms of micelle formation in the solubilization of hydrophobic substances in aqueous solutions.

10. Describe how the Hydrophilic-Lipophilic Balance (HLB) scale is used to optimize the formulation of emulsions in the food and cosmetic industries.

Answer Key for MCQs

1. (B) Cohesion between molecules.
2. (C) Capillarity
3. (B) Newton per meter
4. (D) Boiling Point Elevation Method
5. (B) Chemisorption
6. (C) Surfactants
7. (C) Wettability of the surface
8. (B) Decreases as temperature increases
9. (B) Marangoni Effect - Mass transfer due to tension gradients
10. (C) Reduce surface tension
11. (A) Predicting weather patterns
12. (B) Spinning Drop Method
13. (B) Reducing interfacial tension
14. (B) Pendant Drop Method
15. (C) Surface tension of liquids
16. (C) They stabilize emulsions by reducing interfacial tension.

17.(C) Color of the liquid

18.(B) Physisorption

19.(B) They break down specific types of stains.

20.(A) Hydrophilic-Lipophilic Balance (HLB)

CHAPTER – 5

COMPLEXATION AND PROTEIN BINDING

INTRODUCTION OF COMPLEXATION

Complexation is a fundamental process in chemistry where two or more molecules or ions form a stable association, known as a complex. This process involves the interaction between a central atom or ion, typically a metal, and surrounding molecules or ions, referred to as ligands. The study of complexation is essential for understanding various biological, chemical, and industrial processes.

Types of Complexes

1. **Coordination Complexes:**
   a. **Definition:** These are formed when a central metal ion binds to surrounding ligands through coordinate covalent bonds.
   b. **Example**: The heme group in hemoglobin, where iron (Fe) is the central ion coordinated to nitrogen atoms of porphyrin rings and oxygen molecules.

2. **Inclusion Complexes:**
   a. **Definition:** These complexes involve one molecule (the host) forming a cavity or network that encapsulates another molecule (the guest).
   b. **Example**: Cyclodextrins forming inclusion complexes with various drugs, improving their solubility and stability.

3. **Ion Pairs:**
   a. **Definition**: These are formed between positively charged ions (cations) and negatively charged ions (anions) in solution.
   b. **Example**: Sodium chloride (NaCl) in aqueous solution, where Na+ and Cl- ions associate to form ion pairs.

Factors Affecting Complexation

1. **Nature of the Central Ion:**
   a. **Charge:** The higher the charge on the metal ion, the stronger its attraction to ligands.
   b. **Size:** Smaller ions can accommodate more ligands due to a higher charge density.
   c. **Electronic Configuration**: Influences the geometry and stability of the complex.

2. **Nature of the Ligands:**
   a. **Denticity:** The number of donor atoms in a ligand that can coordinate to the central ion. Ligands can be monodentate, bidentate, or polydentate.
   b. **Charge and Size**: Charged ligands can form stronger electrostatic interactions, and larger ligands might create steric hindrance affecting complex stability.
   c. **Basicity**: More basic ligands tend to form stronger complexes with metal ions.

3. **Environmental Conditions:**
   a. **pH:** Influences the protonation state of ligands and metal ions, affecting complexation.
   b. **Temperature**: Higher temperatures can increase the kinetic energy of molecules, potentially destabilizing complexes.
   c. **Solvent**: The solvent's dielectric constant affects the stability of ionic complexes. Polar solvents can stabilize charged species.

Applications of Complexation

1. **Catalysis:**
   a. **Role:** Metal complexes often serve as catalysts in industrial processes, facilitating reactions by providing an alternative pathway with a lower activation energy.

b. **Example**: Platinum complexes in catalytic converters help reduce vehicle emissions.

2. **Drug Delivery:**

   a. **Role:** Complexation can enhance the solubility, stability, and bioavailability of drugs.

   b. **Example:** Inclusion complexes with cyclodextrins are used to improve the delivery of poorly soluble drugs.

3. **Environmental Chemistry:**

   a. **Role:** Used in the removal and detection of heavy metals and pollutants from water and soil.

   b. **Example**: Chelating agents like EDTA form complexes with heavy metal ions, facilitating their removal from wastewater.

4. **Analytical Chemistry:**

   a. **Role**: Complexation reactions are used in various analytical techniques to detect and quantify metal ions.

   b. **Example**: Colorimetric assays, where metal complexes produce characteristic colors, are used for metal ion detection.

INTRODUCTION OF PROTEIN BINDING

Protein binding is a crucial process in biochemistry where proteins interact with various molecules, which can include other proteins, small molecules (ligands), ions, or even nucleic acids. This interaction is fundamental to numerous biological functions, such as enzyme catalysis, signal transduction, immune responses, and regulation of cellular processes. Understanding protein binding is essential for drug development, disease treatment, and the development of biotechnological applications.

Types of Protein Binding

1. **Reversible Binding:**

   a. **Definition:** Involves non-covalent interactions between the protein and its ligand, which can readily dissociate.

b. **Interactions:** Hydrogen bonds, ionic bonds, van der Waals forces, and hydrophobic interactions.

c. **Example:** The binding of oxygen to hemoglobin, which is reversible and allows for oxygen transport and release.

2. **Irreversible Binding:**

a. **Definition:** Involves covalent bonding between the protein and the ligand, leading to a permanent modification of the protein.

b. **Example**: The binding of aspirin to cyclooxygenase enzymes, which irreversibly inhibits their activity.

Factors Affecting Protein Binding

1. **Concentration of the Binding Partners:**

a. Higher concentrations of proteins and ligands increase the likelihood of interactions, following the principles of mass action.

2. **Affinity:**

a. The strength of the interaction between a protein and its ligand, often quantified by the dissociation constant (Kd). A lower Kd indicates higher affinity.

3. **Conformational Changes:**

a. Binding often induces a conformational change in the protein, which can affect its activity and interaction with other molecules.

4. **Environmental Conditions:**

a. pH, temperature, and ionic strength can influence protein structure and binding affinity. For example, extreme pH levels can denature proteins, affecting binding sites.

Mechanisms of Protein Binding

1. **Lock and Key Model:**

a. **Concept: The** ligand fits precisely into the binding site of the protein, much like a key fits into a lock.

b. **Example**: The specific binding of enzymes to their substrates.

2. **Induced Fit Model:**

   a. **Concept:** The binding of the ligand induces a conformational change in the protein, allowing a tighter fit.

   b. **Example:** The binding of glucose to hexokinase, where the enzyme changes shape to accommodate the glucose molecule.

Applications of Protein Binding

1. **Drug Development:**

   a. **Role**: Understanding how drugs bind to their target proteins helps in designing more effective and selective drugs.

   b. **Example:** Gleevec (imatinib), a drug that specifically binds to the BCR-ABL fusion protein in certain types of cancer, inhibiting its activity.

2. **Diagnostics:**

   a. **Role:** Protein binding assays are used to detect the presence of specific proteins or antibodies in diagnostic tests.

   b. **Example:** ELISA (Enzyme-Linked Immunosorbent Assay) is widely used to detect antigens or antibodies in blood samples.

3. **Biotechnology:**

   a. **Role**: Engineering proteins with specific binding properties for use in biosensors, bioseparation, and therapeutic agents.

   b. **Example**: Monoclonal antibodies designed to bind specific antigens for use in cancer therapy.

Importance in Pharmacokinetics

Protein binding significantly impacts the pharmacokinetics of drugs, influencing their distribution, metabolism, and excretion. Only the unbound fraction of a drug is pharmacologically active, as it can cross cell membranes and interact with its target. Highly protein-bound drugs tend to have a longer duration of action since they are slowly released from the protein complex.

Techniques to Study Protein Binding

1. **Equilibrium Dialysis:**
    a. Measures the binding of small molecules to proteins by separating free and bound ligands through a semi-permeable membrane.
2. **Surface Plasmon Resonance (SPR):**
    a. Provides real-time data on binding kinetics and affinity by measuring changes in refractive index near a sensor surface where binding occurs.
3. **Isothermal Titration Calorimetry (ITC):**
    a. Measures the heat change during binding to determine thermodynamic parameters, including binding affinity and enthalpy.
4. **X-ray Crystallography and NMR Spectroscopy:**
    a. Provide detailed structural information about the protein-ligand complex, revealing the exact nature of the binding interactions.

CLASSIFICATION OF COMPLEXATION

Complexation, the process of forming complexes through the association of two or more molecules or ions, is a fundamental aspect of chemistry that can be classified based on the nature of the interacting species and the type of interactions involved. Understanding these classifications helps in elucidating the behavior and applications of different complexes in biological, chemical, and industrial contexts.

Classification Based on the Nature of the Central Atom/Ion

Complexation involves the formation of a coordination complex where a central atom or ion, usually a metal, is surrounded by a group of molecules or ions, known as ligands. The nature of the central atom or ion is a fundamental factor in determining the properties and types of complexes formed. This classification explores various categories based on the nature of the central atom/ion.

1. Metal Complexes

a. Transition Metal Complexes

1. **Characteristics:** Transition metals (elements in the d-block of the periodic table) form complexes with variable oxidation states and a rich coordination chemistry.

2. **Examples:**

    a. **Iron Complexes**: Hemoglobin (Fe) in blood.

    b. **Copper Complexes**: Copper(II) sulfate complex ($CuSO_4$).

    c. **Platinum Complexes**: Cisplatin (Pt), an anticancer drug.

3. **Significance**: Transition metals have partially filled d-orbitals that can participate in bonding, leading to diverse geometries and reactivity. These complexes are crucial in catalysis, biological systems, and industrial processes.

b. Lanthanide and Actinide Complexes

1. **Characteristics**: Elements from the f-block of the periodic table, characterized by their large atomic and ionic sizes and the presence of 4f and 5f orbitals.

2. **Examples:**

    a. **Lanthanum Complexes**: Lanthanum chloride ($LaCl_3$).

    b. **Uranium Complexes**: Uranyl nitrate ($UO_2(NO_3)_2$).

3. **Significance**: Lanthanides are used in various optical materials and magnets, while actinides are significant in nuclear chemistry and technology.

c. Main Group Metal Complexes

1. **Characteristics**: Metals from the s- and p-blocks of the periodic table, typically forming simpler coordination compounds compared to transition metals.

2. **Examples:**

    a. **Aluminum Complexes**: Aluminum chloride ($AlCl_3$).

    b. **Magnesium Complexes**: Chlorophyll (Mg) in plants.

3. **Significance:** Main group metal complexes are essential in biological systems (e.g., magnesium in chlorophyll) and have applications in materials science and catalysis.

2. Non-Metal Complexes

a. Carbon Complexes

1. **Characteristics:** Complexes where carbon atoms serve as the central atom, commonly seen in organic chemistry.

2. **Examples:**

    a. **Carbenes**: Fischer carbenes ($R_2C=ML\_n$).

    b. **Fullerenes**: C_{60} and its metal complexes.

3. **Significance:** These complexes are important in organic synthesis, materials science, and the development of new carbon-based materials.

b. Silicon Complexes

1. **Characteristics:** Silicon serves as the central atom, forming complexes with various ligands, often seen in organosilicon chemistry.

2. **Examples:**

    a. **Silicones:** Poly(dimethylsiloxane) (PDMS).

    b. **Silicon Carbides**: SiC-based materials.

3. **Significance:** Silicon complexes are widely used in materials science, electronics, and industrial applications due to their thermal stability and unique properties.

3. Bioinorganic Complexes

a. Metal-Enzyme Complexes

1. **Characteristics:** Metal ions are integral components of enzymes, playing crucial roles in catalysis and structural stability.

2. **Examples:**

    a. **Iron in Hemoglobin**: Facilitates oxygen transport in blood.

    b. **Zinc in Carbonic Anhydrase**: Catalyzes the conversion of CO_2 to bicarbonate.

3. **Significance**: Essential for numerous biological processes, these complexes are studied for their roles in health and disease and are targets for drug design.

b. Metal-Nucleic Acid Complexes

1. **Characteristics:** Metal ions interacting with DNA or RNA, affecting their structure and function.

2. **Examples:**

   a. **Cisplatin-DNA Complex**: Platinum-based drug binding to DNA.

   b. **Magnesium-DNA Complex**: Mg^{2+} stabilizing the DNA double helix.

3. **Significance:** These complexes are vital for understanding genetic regulation, gene expression, and the mechanism of action of certain drugs.

Classification Based on the Type of Ligands

Complexation involves the formation of coordination complexes where a central atom or ion is surrounded by ligands, which are molecules or ions that can donate electron pairs to the central atom/ion. Classifying complexation based on the type of ligands provides insights into the diversity and properties of coordination compounds.

1. Inorganic Ligands

a. Monodentate Ligands:

1. **Definition: Ligands** that donate only one electron pair to the central atom/ion.

2. **Examples:** Hydroxide (OH^-), Chloride (Cl^-), Ammonia (NH_3), Cyanide (CN^-).

3. **Characteristics:** Form simple coordination complexes with metal ions, typically resulting in coordination numbers of 2 or 6.

4. **Significance:** Monodentate ligands are common in inorganic chemistry and are used in various industrial processes and coordination polymers.

b. Bidentate Ligands:

1. **Definition: Ligands** that donate two electron pairs to the central atom/ion, forming two bonds.
2. **Examples:** Ethylenediamine (en), Glycinate (gly), Ethylenediaminetetraacetate (EDTA).
3. **Characteristics**: Form chelate complexes with metal ions, increasing their stability and preventing hydrolysis.
4. **Significance**: Bidentate ligands are crucial in metal chelation therapy, catalysis, and analytical chemistry due to their strong and selective binding to metal ions.

c. Polydentate Ligands:

1. **Definition:** Ligands that have multiple donor sites and can form multiple bonds with the central atom/ion.
2. **Examples:** EDTA, DTPA (diethylenetriaminepentaacetate), DOTA (1,4,7,10-tetraazacyclododecane-1,4,7,10-tetraacetic acid).
3. **Characteristic**s: Form highly stable chelate complexes, often used in metal ion sequestration, water treatment, and medical imaging.
4. **Significance:** Polydentate ligands offer enhanced selectivity and efficiency in metal binding compared to monodentate or bidentate ligands.

2. Organic Ligands

a. Aliphatic Ligands:

1. **Definition**: Ligands derived from aliphatic hydrocarbons, often containing linear or branched carbon chains.
2. **Example**s: Ethylenediamine (en), Diethylenetriamine (dien), Triethylenetetramine (trien).
3. **Characteristics**: Flexible ligands that can adopt different conformations, influencing the geometry of the resulting complexes.

4. **Significance**: Aliphatic ligands are widely used in coordination chemistry, particularly in the synthesis of metal complexes and catalysis.

b. Aromatic Ligands:

1. **Definition:** Ligands containing one or more aromatic rings, often with delocalized pi-electron systems.

2. **Examples:** Phenanthroline (phen), Bipyridine (bipy), Anthracene, Benzene derivatives.

3. **Characteristics:** Planar ligands with extended pi-systems, forming stable complexes with metal ions through pi-pi interactions.

4. **Significance**: Aromatic ligands are essential in supramolecular chemistry, molecular recognition, and the design of photoactive materials.

3. Biological Ligands

a. Amino Acids and Peptides:

1. **Definition**: Biomolecules containing an amino group and a carboxyl group, capable of coordinating metal ions.

2. **Examples:** Histidine, Cysteine, Glutathione, Peptides (e.g., Gly-Gly-His).

3. **Characteristics:** Act as biologically relevant ligands in metalloenzymes, metalloproteins, and metallo-drugs, participating in catalysis and structural stabilization.

4. **Significance:** Amino acids and peptides play crucial roles in biological systems, influencing metal homeostasis, signaling pathways, and disease mechanisms.

b. Nucleic Acids:

1. **Definition:** Biopolymers composed of nucleotide monomers (DNA: deoxyribonucleic acid, RNA: ribonucleic acid), capable of binding metal ions.

2. **Examples**: Adenine, Guanine, Thymine, Cytosine, Uracil.

3. **Characteristics:** Serve as ligands for metal ions in DNA/RNA-binding proteins, transcription factors, and metalloenzymes involved in DNA replication and repair.

4. **Significance:** Metal-nucleic acid interactions are essential for DNA structure and stability, gene expression regulation, and therapeutic targeting.

4. Organometallic Ligands

a. Metal Carbonyls:

1. **Definition:** Ligands containing carbon monoxide (CO) coordinated to a metal center through the carbon atom.

2. **Examples: Iron** pentacarbonyl ($Fe(CO)_5$), Nickel tetracarbonyl ($Ni(CO)_4$), Molybdenum hexacarbonyl ($Mo(CO)_6$).

3. **Characteristics:** Form stable complexes with transition metals, often used in organometallic synthesis, catalysis, and industrial processes.

4. **Significance:** Metal carbonyls are important intermediates in organic synthesis and are employed as catalysts in numerous reactions.

b. Metal Alkyls and Aryls:

1. **Definition:** Ligands containing alkyl (R) or aryl (Ar) groups coordinated to a metal center through a carbon-metal bond.

2. **Examples:** Methylcyclopentadienyl manganese tricarbonyl (MMT), Cyclopentadienyliron dicarbonyl dimer (Ferrocene).

3. **Characteristics:** Serve as versatile ligands in organometallic chemistry, exhibiting diverse reactivity and catalytic properties.

4. **Significance:** Metal alkyls and aryls are crucial in homogeneous catalysis, polymerization reactions, and organic synthesis.

Classification Based on the Type of Interaction

Complexation involves the formation of coordination complexes through interactions between a central atom or ion and ligands. Classifying complexation based on the type of interaction provides insights into the nature and properties of coordination compounds. Here are the main categories:

1. Coordination Complexes

a. Covalent Complexes:

1. **Definition**: Formed through sharing of electron pairs between the central atom/ion and ligands.

2. **Characteristics**: Strong directional bonds, often involving ligands with available lone pairs of electrons.

3. **Examples:** Metal carbonyls (e.g., $Fe(CO)_5$), Metal alkyls (e.g., $Ti(CH_3)_4$), Metal hydrides (e.g., Cp_2ZrH_2).

4. **Significance:** Covalent complexes are common in organometallic chemistry and catalysis, exhibiting diverse reactivity and stability.

b. Ionic Complexes:

1. **Definition:** Formed through electrostatic interactions between the central atom/ion and charged ligands.

2. **Characteristics**: Typically involve metal ions with high positive charges and ligands with high negative charges.

3. **Examples**: Metal halides (e.g., $CuCl_2$), Metal oxides (e.g., MgO), Metal phosphates (e.g., $Ca_3(PO_4)_2$).

4. **Significance:** Ionic complexes are important in materials science, solid-state chemistry, and coordination polymers.

2. Non-Covalent Complexes

a. Hydrogen-Bonded Complexes:

1. **Definition:** Formed through hydrogen bonding between hydrogen atoms of ligands and electronegative atoms (e.g., oxygen, nitrogen) of other molecules.

2. **Characteristics:** Weak interactions, typically involving ligands with hydrogen bond donor or acceptor sites.

3. **Examples**: Water clusters, Ammonia complexes, Carboxylic acid dimers.

4. **Significance**: Hydrogen-bonded complexes are crucial in supramolecular chemistry, molecular recognition, and biological systems.

b. π-π Interactions:

1. **Definition:** Arise from stacking interactions between aromatic rings of ligands, leading to delocalization of pi-electrons.
2. **Characteristics**: Weak interactions, significant in ligands with conjugated pi-systems.
3. **Examples**: Aromatic ligands in transition metal complexes (e.g., Phenanthroline, Bipyridine), DNA base stacking.
4. **Significance:** π-π interactions are important in materials science, molecular recognition, and the design of photoactive compounds.

3. Hydrophobic Interactions

a. Hydrophobic Complexes:

1. **Definition:** Arise from the exclusion of non-polar ligands from water, leading to the association of hydrophobic ligands in aqueous environments.
2. **Characteristics**: Weak interactions, driven by entropy considerations.
3. **Examples**: Micelles, Lipid bilayers, Protein-ligand hydrophobic pockets.
4. **Significance:** Hydrophobic interactions play crucial roles in biological processes, drug binding, and the self-assembly of amphiphilic molecules.

4. Metal-Ligand Coordination Interactions

a. Metal-Ligand Coordinate Covalent Bonds:

1. **Definition**: Formed through the sharing of electron pairs between the metal ion and ligand atoms.
2. **Characteristics**: Strong bonds, typically involving ligands with lone pairs of electrons.
3. **Examples**: Coordination complexes with transition metal ions (e.g., $[Fe(CN)_6]^{3-}$), Metalloenzymes (e.g., Hemoglobin).

4. **Significance: Coordinate** covalent bonds are fundamental in coordination chemistry, influencing the stability, geometry, and reactivity of complexes.

b. Metal-Ligand Electrostatic Interactions:

1. **Definition:** Arise from electrostatic attractions between charged metal ions and charged ligands.

2. **Characteristics:** Depend on the charges and distances between metal and ligand atoms.

3. **Examples**: Metal cations with ligands containing anionic groups (e.g., Metal salts, Metal phosphates).

4. **Significance:** Electrostatic interactions are crucial in the binding of metal ions to biological molecules, such as proteins and nucleic acids.

5. Host-Guest Interactions

a. Host-Guest Complexes:

1. **Definition**: Formed between a host molecule (e.g., macrocycle) and a guest molecule that fits into its cavity or binding site.

2. **Characteristic**s: Highly selective interactions, often involving complementary shapes and functional groups.

3. **Examples:** Cyclodextrin inclusion complexes, Calixarene complexes, Cryptand complexes.

4. **Significance:** Host-guest interactions are important in supramolecular chemistry, drug delivery, and molecular recognition.

Classification Based on Function

Complexation plays diverse roles in chemistry, biology, materials science, and various other fields. Classifying complexation based on function provides insights into the specific roles and applications of coordination compounds. Here are the main categories:

1. Catalytic Complexes

a. Homogeneous Catalysis:

1. **Function**: Act as catalysts where both the reactants and catalyst are in the same phase (e.g., liquid or gas).
2. **Examples:** Transition metal complexes like Wilkinson's catalyst ($RhCl(PPh_3)_3$) for hydrogenation reactions, Grubbs' catalyst for olefin metathesis.
3. **Significance**: Homogeneous catalysis is widely used in industrial processes, organic synthesis, and fine chemical production.

b. Heterogeneous Catalysis:

1. **Function:** Act as catalysts where the reactants and catalyst are in different phases (e.g., solid catalyst in a liquid or gas phase).
2. **Examples: Transition** metal oxides (e.g., Fe_2O_3, PtO_2) for industrial processes like ammonia synthesis and catalytic converters.
3. **Significance:** Heterogeneous catalysis is crucial for large-scale industrial reactions, environmental remediation, and energy conversion processes.

2. Sensing and Detection Complexes

a. Chemosensors:

1. **Function**: Bind to specific analytes and undergo a detectable change in properties (e.g., fluorescence, color) upon binding, enabling detection and quantification.
2. **Examples:** Metal complexes with ligands sensitive to pH, metal ions, or biomolecules for environmental monitoring, medical diagnostics, and food safety.
3. **Significance**: Chemosensors are essential tools for analytical chemistry, environmental monitoring, and biomedical applications.

b. Luminescent Probes:

1. **Function:** Emit light (e.g., fluorescence, phosphorescence) upon excitation, allowing for visualization and detection of biological molecules, ions, or environmental factors.

2. **Examples**: Transition metal complexes with luminescent ligands (e.g., $Ru(bpy)_3^{2+}$, $Ir(ppy)_3$) for bioimaging, sensors, and optoelectronic devices.

3. **Significance**: Luminescent probes are valuable for biomedical imaging, molecular diagnostics, and materials science.

3. Therapeutic Complexes

a. Metal-Based Drugs:

1. **Function:** Bind to biological targets (e.g., enzymes, DNA) and exert therapeutic effects, such as anticancer, antimicrobial, or anti-inflammatory activity.

2. **Examples:** Platinum complexes (e.g., cisplatin, carboplatin) for cancer chemotherapy, Ruthenium complexes for photodynamic therapy, Gadolinium complexes for MRI contrast agents.

3. **Significance:** Metal-based drugs offer novel therapeutic strategies for various diseases and have significant potential for personalized medicine.

b. Chelation Therapy Agents:

1. **Function**: Bind to toxic metal ions in the body, forming stable complexes that can be excreted, thereby treating heavy metal poisoning and other metal-related disorders.

2. **Examples:** EDTA (ethylenediaminetetraacetic acid) for lead poisoning, Deferoxamine for iron overload disorders, Succimer for mercury poisoning.

3. **Significance:** Chelation therapy agents are critical for treating acute and chronic metal toxicities and improving patient outcomes.

4. Material Science Complexes

a. Metal-Organic Frameworks (MOFs):

1. **Function**: Serve as porous materials with high surface areas, used for gas storage and separation, catalysis, and drug delivery.

2. **Examples:** Zirconium-based MOFs for gas adsorption, Catalytic MOFs for heterogeneous catalysis, Drug-loaded MOFs for controlled drug release.

3. **Significance:** MOFs are versatile materials with applications in energy storage, environmental remediation, and biomedical engineering.

b. Supramolecular Assemblies:

1. **Function:** Formed through non-covalent interactions, leading to the self-assembly of complex structures with specific properties and functions.

2. **Examples:** Cyclodextrin inclusion complexes, Host-guest assemblies, Self-assembled monolayers (SAMs).

3. **Significance:** Supramolecular assemblies are essential in nanotechnology, surface science, and biomimetic materials design.

5. Biological Complexes

a. Metalloenzymes:

a. **Function:** Incorporate metal ions as cofactors for catalytic activity, enabling various biochemical reactions in living organisms.

b. **Examples:** Hemoglobin (iron-based) for oxygen transport, Carbonic anhydrase (zinc-based) for CO_2 hydration, Cytochrome c oxidase (copper-based) for electron transport.

c. **Significance:** Metalloenzymes are critical for cellular metabolism, respiration, and signaling pathways.

b. Protein-Ligand Complexes:

a. **Function:** Involve the binding of ligands (small molecules, ions) to proteins, modulating their structure and function in biological processes.

b. **Examples:** Drug-protein interactions, Enzyme-substrate complexes, Hormone-receptor complexes.

c. **Significance:** Protein-ligand complexes are central to pharmacology, drug design, and understanding molecular mechanisms of disease.

APPLICATIONS OF COMPLEXATION AND PROTEIN BINDING

Complexation and protein binding are critical processes that have vast applications across various fields including medicine, environmental science, biotechnology, and industrial processes. Understanding these interactions allows for the development of new technologies, improvement of existing methods, and better comprehension of biological systems.

Applications of Complexation

Complexation, the formation of coordination complexes between a central atom or ion and ligands, finds wide-ranging applications across various fields due to its diverse properties and functionalities. Here are some key applications:

1. Catalysis

a. Homogeneous Catalysis:

1. Transition metal complexes serve as catalysts in numerous organic transformations, such as hydrogenation, oxidation, and cross-coupling reactions.

2. Examples include Wilkinson's catalyst $(RhCl(PPh_3)_3)$ for olefin hydrogenation and Grubbs' catalyst for olefin metathesis.

b. Heterogeneous Catalysis:

1. Metal complexes immobilized on solid supports catalyze industrial processes like ammonia synthesis, petroleum refining, and environmental remediation.

2. Metal oxides (e.g., Fe_2O_3, PtO_2) and zeolites are widely used heterogeneous catalysts.

2. Sensing and Detection

a. Chemosensors:

1. Metal complexes with specific ligands undergo detectable changes (e.g., fluorescence, color) upon binding to target analytes, enabling their detection and quantification.

2. Chemosensors are vital in environmental monitoring, medical diagnostics, and food safety.

b. Luminescent Probes:

1. Transition metal complexes with luminescent ligands are used as probes for bioimaging, sensors, and optoelectronic devices.

2. These probes offer high sensitivity and selectivity for detecting biological molecules and environmental factors.

3. Drug Design and Therapeutics

a. Metal-Based Drugs:

1. Transition metal complexes exhibit promising therapeutic properties, particularly in cancer chemotherapy, where platinum-based drugs like cisplatin and carboplatin are widely used.

2. Other metal complexes, such as ruthenium and gold compounds, show potential as anticancer agents.

b. Chelation Therapy Agents:

1. Complexing agents like EDTA and deferoxamine are employed in chelation therapy to treat heavy metal poisoning and metal-related disorders by sequestering toxic metal ions and facilitating their excretion.

4. Material Science

a. Metal-Organic Frameworks (MOFs):

1. MOFs are porous materials with high surface areas, used for gas storage and separation, catalysis, drug delivery, and sensing applications.

2. Their tunable properties make them attractive for various industrial and environmental applications.

b. Supramolecular Assemblies:

1. Complexation-driven self-assembly processes lead to the formation of supramolecular structures with specific properties, such as cyclodextrin inclusion complexes and host-guest assemblies.

2. These assemblies are utilized in nanotechnology, molecular recognition, and biomaterials design.

5. Biological Applications

a. Metalloenzymes:

1. Metal ions serve as essential cofactors in metalloenzymes, enabling catalytic activity in various biochemical reactions.
2. Examples include hemoglobin (iron-based) for oxygen transport and carbonic anhydrase (zinc-based) for CO_2 hydration.

b. Protein-Ligand Interactions:

1. Complexation between proteins and ligands plays a crucial role in pharmacology, drug design, and understanding molecular mechanisms of disease.
2. Protein-ligand complexes are targets for drug development and are studied extensively in structural biology and medicinal chemistry.

6. Environmental Applications

a. Heavy Metal Remediation:

1. Chelating agents and complexing agents are employed in environmental remediation to sequester and remove toxic heavy metal ions from soil, water, and wastewater.
2. EDTA, citrate, and humic substances are commonly used in metal ion chelation and soil stabilization.

b. Water Treatment:

1. Complexation processes are utilized in water treatment for metal ion removal, precipitation, and purification.
2. Chemical agents like polyphosphates and polyacrylates form complexes with metal ions, facilitating their removal through precipitation or filtration.

Applications of Protein Binding

Protein binding, the interaction between proteins and other molecules, is a crucial process with widespread applications across various fields. Here are some key applications:

1. Drug Discovery and Development

a. Drug Targeting:

1. Understanding protein-ligand interactions aids in the design of drugs that target specific proteins involved in diseases. By binding to target proteins, drugs can modulate their activity, leading to therapeutic effects.
2. Rational drug design relies on computational methods, such as molecular docking and virtual screening, to predict and optimize protein-ligand interactions.

b. Pharmacokinetics and Pharmacodynamics:

1. Protein binding influences the distribution, metabolism, and elimination of drugs in the body. High protein binding can extend a drug's half-life by reducing its clearance rate and increasing its plasma concentration.
2. Protein binding also affects a drug's pharmacodynamic properties, influencing its efficacy and potency in interacting with target proteins.

2. Biomolecular Interactions and Signaling Pathways

a. Signal Transduction:

1. Protein binding plays a central role in cellular signaling pathways, where proteins interact with ligands, receptors, and other signaling molecules to transmit extracellular signals into intracellular responses.
2. Examples include ligand-receptor interactions in hormone signaling pathways (e.g., insulin signaling) and protein-protein interactions in kinase cascades.

b. Protein-Protein Interactions:

1. Understanding protein-protein interactions is essential for elucidating biological processes, such as protein folding, assembly of macromolecular complexes, and regulation of gene expression.

2. Techniques like yeast two-hybrid assays, co-immunoprecipitation, and surface plasmon resonance (SPR) spectroscopy are used to study protein-protein interactions.

3. Biomolecular Sensing and Diagnostics

a. Biosensors:

1. Protein binding is exploited in biosensors for the detection and quantification of biomolecules, toxins, pathogens, and environmental contaminants.
2. Biosensors employ various transduction mechanisms, such as optical, electrochemical, and piezoelectric, to convert protein-ligand interactions into measurable signals.

b. Immunoassays:

1. Immunoassays utilize protein binding, particularly antigen-antibody interactions, for the detection of specific proteins (e.g., hormones, antibodies, tumor markers) in biological samples.
2. Enzyme-linked immunosorbent assay (ELISA), Western blotting, and immunohistochemistry are common immunoassay techniques used in research and clinical diagnostics.

4. Biotechnology and Protein Engineering

a. Protein Purification:

1. Protein-ligand interactions are exploited in chromatographic techniques for protein purification, where target proteins bind selectively to ligands immobilized on chromatography matrices.
2. Affinity chromatography, ion exchange chromatography, and size exclusion chromatography are widely used for protein purification.

b. Protein Engineering:

1. Rational design and directed evolution of proteins rely on understanding and manipulating protein-ligand interactions to modulate protein function, stability, and specificity.

2. Applications include the engineering of enzymes with enhanced catalytic activity, antibodies with improved binding affinity, and receptors with altered ligand specificity.

5. Structural Biology and Drug Target Identification

a. Protein Structure Determination:

1. Protein-ligand complexes are studied using structural biology techniques, such as X-ray crystallography, nuclear magnetic resonance (NMR) spectroscopy, and cryo-electron microscopy, to elucidate their three-dimensional structures and binding interfaces.

2. Structural information guides drug discovery efforts by providing insights into protein-ligand interactions and potential binding sites.

b. Virtual Screening and Structure-Based Drug Design:

1. Computational methods, including molecular docking, molecular dynamics simulations, and structure-based virtual screening, are employed to identify and optimize small molecules that bind to target proteins.

2. Structure-based drug design exploits protein-ligand interactions to develop novel therapeutics with improved potency, selectivity, and pharmacokinetic properties.

6. Environmental Monitoring and Bioremediation

a. Biosorption and Bioremediation:

1. Proteins, such as enzymes and microbial surface proteins, bind to environmental pollutants, heavy metals, and toxins, facilitating their removal from water and soil through processes like biosorption and bioremediation.

2. Bioremediation strategies leverage protein-ligand interactions to remediate contaminated environments and mitigate pollution.

b. Biomimetic Sensors:

1. Protein-based sensors and biomimetic materials inspired by protein-ligand interactions are developed for environmental monitoring, detecting pollutants, and assessing water quality.

2. These biomimetic sensors mimic the specificity and selectivity of natural protein receptors for target analytes.

Integrated Applications of Complexation and Protein Binding

1. **Metalloproteins:**
   a. **Role:** Study of metal complexes within proteins (metalloproteins) to understand their function in biological systems.
   b. **Example:** Hemoglobin's iron complex binds oxygen for transport in the blood.
   c. **Impact:** Provides insights into essential biological processes and informs the development of biomimetic materials.

2. **Biosensors:**
   a. **Role**: Combining complexation and protein binding principles to develop sensitive and selective biosensors.
   b. **Example:** Glucose sensors using enzymes like glucose oxidase that bind glucose and produce a detectable signal.
   c. **Impact**: Facilitates real-time monitoring of biological parameters, improving disease management and health monitoring.

3. **Theranostics:**
   a. **Role:** Integrating therapeutic and diagnostic applications through complexation and protein binding.
   b. **Example**: Nanoparticles designed to target cancer cells and deliver drugs while also enabling imaging for diagnosis.
   c. **Impact:** Offers a comprehensive approach to disease treatment and monitoring, enhancing personalized medicine.

Methods of analysis

Analyzing complexation and protein binding interactions is essential for understanding their mechanisms, stability, and applications. Several sophisticated techniques are employed to study these interactions, each with its strengths and specific applications.

Methods of Analysis in Complexation

Analyzing complexation reactions and protein-ligand interactions involves a variety of experimental and computational techniques. Here are some commonly used methods:

1. Spectroscopic Techniques

a. UV-Visible Spectroscopy:

1. **Principle**: Measures the absorbance of light in the ultraviolet-visible range (200-800 nm) by chromophores present in the complex.

2. **Applications**: Determination of complex formation constants, monitoring ligand binding to metal ions, and studying electronic transitions in coordination complexes.

b. Fluorescence Spectroscopy:

1. **Principle:** Measures the emission of fluorescence upon excitation of fluorophores in the complex.

2. **Applications**: Monitoring protein-ligand interactions, studying conformational changes in biomolecules, and detecting ligand binding to receptors.

c. Circular Dichroism (CD) Spectroscopy:

1. **Principle:** Measures the differential absorption of left and right circularly polarized light by chiral molecules.

2. **Applications**: Characterizing the secondary structure of proteins, studying protein folding/unfolding, and monitoring ligand-induced conformational changes.

2. Nuclear Magnetic Resonance (NMR) Spectroscopy

a. 1D and 2D NMR Spectroscopy:

1. **Principle:** Analyzes the interactions between atomic nuclei and magnetic fields, providing structural and dynamic information about molecules.

2. **Applications**: Determining the structure of complex molecules, elucidating protein-ligand binding modes, and studying protein dynamics.

3. Mass Spectrometry (MS)

a. Electrospray Ionization Mass Spectrometry (ESI-MS):

1. **Principle:** Ionizes molecules in solution and analyzes their mass-to-charge ratio (m/z).

2. **Applications**: Identifying and characterizing complex molecules, determining stoichiometry of protein-ligand complexes, and studying protein modifications.

b. Matrix-Assisted Laser Desorption/Ionization Mass Spectrometry (MALDI-MS):

1. **Principle**: Generates gas-phase ions of large molecules by desorption and ionization using a laser and a matrix compound.

2. **Applications**: Analyzing biomolecules, such as proteins and nucleic acids, determining protein-ligand binding affinities, and identifying post-translational modifications.

4. X-ray Crystallography

a. Protein Crystallography:

1. **Principle**: Determines the three-dimensional structure of proteins by analyzing the diffraction patterns of X-rays scattered by protein crystals.

2. **Applications**: Elucidating protein-ligand binding modes, identifying active sites, and understanding the structural basis of enzyme catalysis.

5. Surface Plasmon Resonance (SPR)

a. Surface Plasmon Resonance Spectroscopy:

1. **Principle**: Measures changes in refractive index near a metal surface caused by biomolecular interactions, providing real-time kinetic and affinity data.

2. **Applications**: Studying protein-protein interactions, characterizing ligand binding kinetics, and screening small molecule inhibitors.

6. Isothermal Titration Calorimetry (ITC)

a. Isothermal Titration Calorimetry:

1. **Principle:** Measures the heat released or absorbed during a binding reaction, allowing determination of binding stoichiometry, affinity, and thermodynamics.

2. **Applications**: Quantifying protein-ligand binding constants, determining binding energetics, and studying ligand-induced conformational changes.

7. Computational Methods

a. Molecular Docking:

1. **Principle**: Predicts the preferred binding modes and affinities of small molecules to protein targets using computational algorithms and structural information.

2. **Applications**: Virtual screening of compound libraries, predicting ligand-protein interactions, and guiding structure-based drug design.

b. Molecular Dynamics (MD) Simulations:

1. **Principle**: Simulates the dynamic behavior of molecules over time using classical or quantum mechanical force fields.

2. **Applications**: Studying protein-ligand interactions at atomic resolution, elucidating binding mechanisms, and exploring protein conformational dynamics.

Methods of Analysis in Protein Binding

Analyzing protein-ligand interactions, a fundamental aspect of complexation, involves various experimental and computational techniques. Here are some commonly used methods:

Experimental Techniques

1. Surface Plasmon Resonance (SPR)

a. **Principle**: Measures changes in the refractive index near a metal surface caused by biomolecular interactions, providing real-time kinetic and affinity data.

b. **Applications:** Studying protein-ligand interactions, characterizing binding kinetics, and screening small molecule inhibitors.

2. Isothermal Titration Calorimetry (ITC)

a. **Principle**: Measures the heat released or absorbed during a binding reaction, enabling determination of binding stoichiometry, affinity, and thermodynamics.

b. **Applications**: Quantifying protein-ligand binding constants, determining binding energetics, and studying ligand-induced conformational changes.

3. Fluorescence Spectroscopy

a. **Principle:** Measures changes in fluorescence intensity or emission spectra of fluorophores upon ligand binding to proteins.

b. **Applications:** Monitoring protein-ligand interactions, studying conformational changes in biomolecules, and quantifying binding affinities.

4. Circular Dichroism (CD) Spectroscopy

a. **Principle:** Measures the differential absorption of left and right circularly polarized light by chiral molecules, providing information about protein secondary structure and folding.

b. **Applications**: Studying protein conformational changes upon ligand binding, characterizing protein stability, and determining binding stoichiometry.

5. Nuclear Magnetic Resonance (NMR) Spectroscopy

a. **Principle:** Analyzes interactions between atomic nuclei and magnetic fields, providing structural and dynamic information about proteins and their ligands.

b. **Applications:** Determining the structure of protein-ligand complexes, mapping binding interfaces, and studying ligand-induced conformational changes.

6. X-ray Crystallography

a. **Principle**: Determines the three-dimensional structure of proteins and protein-ligand complexes by analyzing X-ray diffraction patterns from protein crystals.

b. **Applications:** Elucidating detailed molecular structures, identifying binding sites, and understanding the structural basis of protein-ligand interactions.

Computational Techniques

1. Molecular Docking

a. **Principle**: Predicts the preferred binding modes and affinities of small molecules to protein targets using computational algorithms and structural information.

b. **Applications**: Virtual screening of compound libraries, predicting ligand-protein interactions, and guiding structure-based drug design.

2. Molecular Dynamics (MD) Simulations

a. **Principle: Simulates** the dynamic behavior of proteins and their ligands over time using classical or quantum mechanical force fields.

b. **Applications**: Studying protein-ligand interactions at atomic resolution, elucidating binding mechanisms, and exploring ligand-induced conformational changes.

3. Quantitative Structure-Activity Relationship (QSAR) Analysis

a. **Principle**: Correlates the chemical structure of ligands with their biological activity through statistical models and computational algorithms.

b. **Applications**: Predicting ligand binding affinities, identifying structure-activity relationships, and optimizing lead compounds in drug discovery.

4. Binding Free Energy Calculations

a. **Principle:** Calculates the change in free energy associated with protein-ligand binding using molecular mechanics and statistical mechanics approaches.

b. **Applications**: Predicting binding affinities, ranking ligands by potency, and designing novel ligands with improved binding properties.

PROTEIN BINDING

Protein binding is a critical biochemical process where proteins interact with various molecules, which can include other proteins, small molecules (ligands), ions, or nucleic acids. These interactions are essential for numerous biological functions such as enzymatic activity, signal transduction, immune responses, and cellular regulation. The study of protein binding provides insights into how proteins function and interact within biological systems and has significant applications in drug development, diagnostics, and biotechnology.

Mechanisms of Protein Binding

a. Protein binding, a crucial aspect of complexation, involves various mechanisms through which proteins interact with other molecules, including small ligands, ions, peptides, and other proteins. Here are some common mechanisms of protein binding:

1. Lock-and-Key Model

a. **Principle:** In the lock-and-key model, the protein's binding site (the lock) has a specific shape and chemical properties complementary to those of the ligand (the key). The ligand fits into the binding site with high specificity and affinity.

b. **Applications**: This mechanism is common in enzyme-substrate interactions, where enzymes recognize and bind specific substrates based on their complementary shapes and chemical features.

2. Induced Fit Model

a. **Principle**: In the induced fit model, the protein's binding site undergoes conformational changes upon ligand binding, leading to a more optimal fit between the protein and ligand. Both the protein and ligand adapt their conformations to maximize binding affinity.

b. **Applications**: This mechanism is observed in many protein-ligand interactions, where the binding event induces structural changes in the protein, leading to tighter binding and functional modulation.

3. Hydrophobic Interactions

a. **Principle:** Hydrophobic interactions occur between nonpolar regions of the protein and hydrophobic groups on the ligand. These interactions are driven by the tendency of hydrophobic molecules to minimize their contact with water molecules.

b. **Applications**: Hydrophobic interactions play a significant role in stabilizing protein-ligand complexes, particularly in the binding of nonpolar ligands to hydrophobic pockets within proteins.

4. Electrostatic Interactions

a. **Principle**: Electrostatic interactions involve the attraction or repulsion between charged groups on the protein and ligand. These interactions can be attractive (e.g., between oppositely charged groups) or repulsive (e.g., between similarly charged groups).

b. **Applications**: Electrostatic interactions contribute to the overall binding affinity of protein-ligand complexes and are particularly important in the binding of ions, charged molecules, and proteins with charged domains.

5. Hydrogen Bonding

a. **Principle**: Hydrogen bonding occurs between hydrogen atoms of the protein and electronegative atoms (e.g., oxygen, nitrogen) of the ligand. Hydrogen bonds are relatively strong and directional, contributing to the specificity and stability of protein-ligand complexes.

b. **Applications:** Hydrogen bonding plays a crucial role in molecular recognition, where specific hydrogen bond donors and acceptors on the protein and ligand interact to form stable complexes.

6. Van der Waals Interactions

a. **Principle**: Van der Waals interactions are weak, nonspecific forces that arise from fluctuations in electron density within molecules. These interactions include dispersion forces, dipole-dipole interactions, and induced dipole interactions.

b. **Applications:** Van der Waals interactions contribute to the overall stability of protein-ligand complexes by providing additional attractive forces between nonpolar regions of the protein and ligand.

7. Covalent Bonding

a. **Principle**: In some cases, proteins can form covalent bonds with ligands through nucleophilic or electrophilic reactions. Covalent binding typically involves the formation of a stable chemical bond between a reactive group on the protein and a reactive group on the ligand.

b. **Applications:** Covalent binding can lead to irreversible inhibition of enzymes or specific targeting of proteins for therapeutic purposes.

Factors Influencing Protein Binding

Protein binding, a critical aspect of complexation, is influenced by various factors that govern the interaction between proteins and other molecules. Understanding these factors is essential for predicting and manipulating protein-ligand interactions. Here are some key factors that influence protein binding:

1. Molecular Structure and Shape

a. **Complementary Binding Surfaces**: Proteins and ligands often have complementary shapes and chemical features, facilitating specific binding interactions.

b. **Binding Site Accessibility**: The accessibility of the protein's binding site, determined by its structural conformation and flexibility, affects ligand binding affinity and kinetics.

2. Chemical Composition and Properties

a. **Hydrophobicity**: Hydrophobic interactions play a significant role in protein-ligand binding, with hydrophobic regions of the protein and ligand associating to minimize exposure to water molecules.

b. **Electrostatic Interactions**: Electrostatic attractions or repulsions between charged groups on the protein and ligand influence binding affinity, particularly for ions and charged molecules.

c. **Hydrogen Bonding**: Hydrogen bonds formed between protein and ligand contribute to the specificity and stability of the complex, particularly for interactions involving polar groups.

3. Binding Site Flexibility and Dynamics

a. **Induced Fit**: Proteins may undergo conformational changes upon ligand binding, resulting in an optimized fit between the protein and ligand and enhancing binding affinity.

b. **Allosteric Effects**: Ligand binding at one site on the protein may induce conformational changes at distant sites (allosteric sites), modulating protein function and ligand binding affinity.

4. Protein-Ligand Concentrations

a. **Ligand Concentration**: Increasing ligand concentration typically increases the probability of binding to the protein, leading to higher binding affinity and saturation of binding sites.

b. **Protein Concentration**: Higher protein concentrations can enhance binding affinity through increased chances of encountering ligands and occupancy of available binding sites.

5. pH and Ionic Strength

a. **pH**: Changes in pH can affect the ionization states of amino acid residues in the protein's binding site, influencing electrostatic interactions and binding affinity.

b. **Ionic Strength**: Salt concentrations in the surrounding solution can alter protein stability, conformation, and electrostatic interactions, thereby affecting binding affinity.

6. Temperature and Environmental Conditions

a. **Temperature**: Changes in temperature can affect protein stability, dynamics, and conformational flexibility, influencing binding affinity and kinetics.

b. **Solvent Conditions**: Environmental factors such as solvent polarity, viscosity, and dielectric constant can influence protein-ligand interactions by affecting the hydration shell and solvent accessibility of the binding site.

7. Post-Translational Modifications (PTMs)

a. Phosphorylation, Acetylation, Glycosylation, etc.: PTMs can modulate protein structure, function, and binding properties, altering protein-ligand interactions and cellular signaling pathways.

8. Binding Cooperativity and Multivalency

a. **Cooperativity**: Cooperative binding occurs when ligand binding at one site influences the binding affinity at other sites on the protein, leading to enhanced or reduced affinity.

b. **Multivalency**: Multivalent ligands or proteins with multiple binding sites can exhibit enhanced binding affinity and selectivity through simultaneous interactions with multiple binding sites on the protein.

Types of Protein Binding Interactions

Protein binding involves various types of interactions between proteins and other molecules, including small ligands, ions, peptides, and other proteins. These interactions are essential for molecular recognition, signaling, catalysis, and structural stability. Here are some common types of protein binding interactions:

1. Hydrophobic Interactions

a. **Principle:** Hydrophobic interactions occur between nonpolar regions of the protein and hydrophobic groups on the ligand. These interactions are driven by the tendency of hydrophobic molecules to minimize their contact with water molecules.

b. **Applications:** Hydrophobic interactions play a significant role in stabilizing protein-ligand complexes, particularly in the binding of nonpolar ligands to hydrophobic pockets within proteins.

2. Electrostatic Interactions

a. **Principle:** Electrostatic interactions involve the attraction or repulsion between charged groups on the protein and ligand. These interactions can be attractive (e.g., between oppositely charged groups) or repulsive (e.g., between similarly charged groups).

b. **Applications:** Electrostatic interactions contribute to the overall binding affinity of protein-ligand complexes and are particularly important in the binding of ions, charged molecules, and proteins with charged domains.

3. Hydrogen Bonding

a. **Principle:** Hydrogen bonding occurs between hydrogen atoms of the protein and electronegative atoms (e.g., oxygen, nitrogen) of the ligand. Hydrogen bonds are relatively strong and directional, contributing to the specificity and stability of protein-ligand complexes.

b. **Applications:** Hydrogen bonding plays a crucial role in molecular recognition, where specific hydrogen bond donors and acceptors on the protein and ligand interact to form stable complexes.

4. Van der Waals Interactions

a. **Principle:** Van der Waals interactions are weak, nonspecific forces that arise from fluctuations in electron density within molecules. These interactions include dispersion forces, dipole-dipole interactions, and induced dipole interactions.

b. **Applications:** Van der Waals interactions contribute to the overall stability of protein-ligand complexes by providing additional attractive forces between nonpolar regions of the protein and ligand.

5. Ionic Interactions

a. **Principle**: Ionic interactions involve the attraction between positively and negatively charged ions or ionizable groups on the protein and ligand.

b. **Applications**: Ionic interactions contribute to the overall stability and specificity of protein-ligand complexes, particularly in the binding of ions, charged molecules, and proteins with charged domains.

6. Covalent Bonding

a. **Principle**: In some cases, proteins can form covalent bonds with ligands through nucleophilic or electrophilic reactions. Covalent binding typically involves the formation of a stable chemical bond between a reactive group on the protein and a reactive group on the ligand.

b. **Applications**: Covalent binding can lead to irreversible inhibition of enzymes or specific targeting of proteins for therapeutic purposes.

Applications of Protein Binding

1. **Drug Development:**
   a. **Role:** Understanding protein-ligand interactions is crucial for designing drugs that specifically target biological pathways.
   b. **Example**: Gleevec (imatinib) specifically binds to the BCR-ABL fusion protein in chronic myeloid leukemia, inhibiting its activity.
   c. **Impact:** Leads to the creation of highly specific and effective therapeutics with reduced side effects.

2. **Diagnostics:**

a. **Role:** Protein binding assays are used to detect the presence of specific proteins, antibodies, or other biomolecules in diagnostic tests.

b. **Example**: ELISA (Enzyme-Linked Immunosorbent Assay) detects antigens or antibodies in blood samples.

c. **Impact**: Provides sensitive and specific methods for disease diagnosis, improving early detection and treatment outcomes.

3. **Biotechnology:**

a. **Role**: Engineered proteins with specific binding properties are used in various biotechnological applications.

b. **Example:** Monoclonal antibodies designed to bind specific antigens are used in cancer therapy and as diagnostic tools.

c. **Impact:** Advances in biotechnology lead to novel therapeutic and diagnostic tools, enhancing medical care and research capabilities.

4. **Pharmacokinetics:**

a. **Role**: Protein binding affects the distribution, metabolism, and excretion of drugs within the body.

b. **Example**: Highly protein-bound drugs like warfarin have prolonged action due to slow release from protein complexes.

c. **Impact**: Understanding protein binding properties helps in designing drugs with optimal efficacy and safety profiles.

5. **Structural Biology:**

a. **Role**: Studying protein-ligand complexes provides insights into the structure and function of biological macromolecules.

b. **Example**: X-ray crystallography and NMR spectroscopy reveal the detailed structures of enzyme-substrate complexes.

c. **Impact**: Enhances our understanding of biochemical processes and aids in the design of inhibitors and other therapeutic agents.

Methods of Analyzing Protein Binding

Analyzing protein binding, a fundamental aspect of complexation, involves a variety of experimental and computational techniques. These methods provide insights into the interactions between proteins and other molecules, such as small ligands, ions, peptides, and other proteins. Here are some common methods used to analyze protein binding:

Experimental Techniques

1. Surface Plasmon Resonance (SPR)

a. **Principle**: Measures changes in the refractive index near a metal surface caused by biomolecular interactions, providing real-time kinetic and affinity data.

b. **Applications:** Studying protein-ligand interactions, characterizing binding kinetics, and screening small molecule inhibitors.

2. Isothermal Titration Calorimetry (ITC)

a. **Principle**: Measures the heat released or absorbed during a binding reaction, enabling determination of binding stoichiometry, affinity, and thermodynamics.

b. **Applications:** Quantifying protein-ligand binding constants, determining binding energetics, and studying ligand-induced conformational changes.

3. Fluorescence Spectroscopy

a. **Principle**: Measures changes in fluorescence intensity or emission spectra of fluorophores upon ligand binding to proteins.

b. **Applications:** Monitoring protein-ligand interactions, studying conformational changes in biomolecules, and quantifying binding affinities.

4. Circular Dichroism (CD) Spectroscopy

a. **Principle:** Measures the differential absorption of left and right circularly polarized light by chiral molecules, providing information about protein secondary structure and folding.

b. **Applications**: Studying protein conformational changes upon ligand binding, characterizing protein stability, and determining binding stoichiometry.

5. Nuclear Magnetic Resonance (NMR) Spectroscopy

a. **Principle**: Analyzes interactions between atomic nuclei and magnetic fields, providing structural and dynamic information about proteins and their ligands.

b. **Applications**: Determining the structure of protein-ligand complexes, mapping binding interfaces, and studying ligand-induced conformational changes.

6. X-ray Crystallography

a. **Principle**: Determines the three-dimensional structure of proteins and protein-ligand complexes by analyzing X-ray diffraction patterns from protein crystals.

b. **Applications**: Elucidating detailed molecular structures, identifying binding sites, and understanding the structural basis of protein-ligand interactions.

Computational Techniques

1. Molecular Docking

a. **Principle**: Predicts the preferred binding modes and affinities of small molecules to protein targets using computational algorithms and structural information.

b. **Applications**: Virtual screening of compound libraries, predicting ligand-protein interactions, and guiding structure-based drug design.

2. Molecular Dynamics (MD) Simulations

a. **Principle:** Simulates the dynamic behavior of proteins and their ligands over time using classical or quantum mechanical force fields.

b. **Applications:** Studying protein-ligand interactions at atomic resolution, elucidating binding mechanisms, and exploring ligand-induced conformational changes.

3. **Quantitative Structure-Activity Relationship (QSAR) Analysis**

   a. **Principle:** Correlates the chemical structure of ligands with their biological activity through statistical models and computational algorithms.

   b. **Applications**: Predicting ligand binding affinities, identifying structure-activity relationships, and optimizing lead compounds in drug discovery.

4. **Binding Free Energy Calculations**

   a. **Principle**: Calculates the change in free energy associated with protein-ligand binding using molecular mechanics and statistical mechanics approaches.

   b. **Applications**: Predicting binding affinities, ranking ligands by potency, and designing novel ligands with improved binding properties.

Complexation and drug action

Complexation and protein binding play pivotal roles in the pharmacokinetics and pharmacodynamics of drugs. Understanding these interactions is essential for designing effective drugs with optimal therapeutic effects and minimal side effects. This section explores the interplay between complexation and drug action, detailing how these processes influence drug behavior and efficacy.

Role of Complexation in Drug Action

1. **Improving Drug Solubility:**

   a. **Mechanism**: Many drugs have poor water solubility, which can be improved through complexation with solubilizing agents.

   b. **Example:** Cyclodextrins form inclusion complexes with hydrophobic drugs, increasing their aqueous solubility.

c. **Impact**: Enhanced solubility leads to improved bioavailability, allowing for more efficient drug absorption and effectiveness.

2. **Enhancing Drug Stability:**

   a. **Mechanism**: Complexation can protect drugs from degradation by stabilizing the active form against environmental factors like light, oxygen, and enzymes.

   b. **Example:** Metal complexes like cisplatin, where the platinum ion stabilizes the drug structure, protecting it from premature degradation.

   c. **Impact:** Increased stability prolongs the shelf-life and therapeutic efficacy of the drug.

3. **Controlled Drug Release:**

   a. **Mechanism**: Complexation can provide a mechanism for sustained or controlled release of drugs, maintaining therapeutic levels over an extended period.

   b. **Example:** Drug-polymer complexes where the drug is released slowly as the polymer matrix degrades.

   c. **Impact:** Controlled release reduces dosing frequency, improves patient compliance, and minimizes side effects associated with peak drug concentrations.

4. **Targeted Drug Delivery:**

   a. **Mechanism:** Complexation with targeting ligands can direct drugs to specific tissues or cells, enhancing efficacy and reducing systemic toxicity.

   b. **Example:** Liposomal drug delivery systems where drugs are encapsulated in liposomes decorated with antibodies or ligands targeting cancer cells.

   c. **Impact:** Increased drug concentration at the target site improves therapeutic outcomes and reduces off-target effects.

5. **Reducing Drug Toxicity:**

a. **Mechanism**: Complexation can minimize drug toxicity by altering the distribution and reducing the concentration of free drug in systemic circulation.

b. **Example**: Chelation therapy for heavy metal poisoning, where chelating agents form complexes with toxic metals, facilitating their excretion.

c. **Impact:** Enhanced safety profile and reduced risk of adverse effects.

Role of Protein Binding in Drug Action

1. **Drug Distribution:**

   a. **Mechanism**: The extent of protein binding affects the distribution of drugs within the body. Highly bound drugs are often confined to the vascular system, while free drugs can diffuse into tissues.

   b. **Example**: Warfarin is highly bound to plasma proteins, limiting its distribution to the extracellular fluid and maintaining its anticoagulant effect.

   c. **Impact**: Understanding protein binding helps predict drug distribution and optimize dosing regimens.

2. **Drug Metabolism:**

   a. **Mechanism**: Protein binding can protect drugs from rapid metabolism by sequestering them from metabolic enzymes.

   b. **Example**: Drugs like ibuprofen bind to plasma proteins, reducing their immediate availability for metabolism by liver enzymes.

   c. **Impact:** Modulating drug metabolism can enhance therapeutic duration and effectiveness.

3. **Drug Excretion:**

   a. **Mechanism**: The bound fraction of a drug is usually not filtered by the kidneys, affecting the drug's excretion rate.

   b. **Example**: Highly protein-bound drugs like diazepam have slower renal excretion rates, prolonging their half-life in the body.

c. **Impact:** Influences the design of dosing schedules to maintain therapeutic drug levels.

4. **Drug-Drug Interactions:**

    a. **Mechanism**: Drugs can compete for binding sites on plasma proteins, leading to displacement and altered effects.

    b. **Example**: Sulfonamides can displace warfarin from its binding sites, increasing the concentration of free warfarin and enhancing its anticoagulant effect.

    c. **Impact**: Knowledge of binding interactions is crucial for avoiding adverse drug interactions and ensuring safe polypharmacy practices.

5. **Pharmacodynamics:**

    a. **Mechanism**: The free (unbound) drug concentration correlates with pharmacological activity since only free drug can cross cell membranes and interact with target receptors.

    b. **Example:** The free fraction of antibiotics determines their antimicrobial activity against pathogens.

    c. **Impact**: Optimizing free drug levels is key to achieving desired therapeutic outcomes.

Analytical Techniques for Studying Complexation and Protein Binding in Drug Action

1. **Surface Plasmon Resonance (SPR):**

    a. **Application:** Real-time analysis of drug-protein interactions to determine binding kinetics and affinity.

    b. **Example:** Studying the binding of small molecules to albumin.

2. **Isothermal Titration Calorimetry (ITC):**

    a. **Application**: Measuring the thermodynamics of drug binding to proteins, providing insights into binding affinity and enthalpy changes.

b. **Example**: Analyzing the binding of antiretroviral drugs to HIV protease.

3. **X-ray Crystallography:**
   a. **Application**: Determining the three-dimensional structures of drug-protein complexes at atomic resolution.
   b. **Example**: Elucidating the binding mode of kinase inhibitors to their targets.

4. **Nuclear Magnetic Resonance (NMR) Spectroscopy:**
   a. **Application**: Providing detailed structural and dynamic information about drug-protein interactions in solution.
   b. **Example**: Investigating the binding sites of allosteric modulators on receptors.

5. **Mass Spectrometry (MS):**
   a. **Application: Identifying** and quantifying drug-protein complexes, and studying their stoichiometry.
   b. **Example**: Using native MS to study the interaction of monoclonal antibodies **with antigens.**

6. **Equilibrium Dialysis:**
   a. **Application**: Determining the extent of drug binding to plasma proteins by measuring free and bound drug concentrations.
   b. **Example**: Assessing the binding of anticoagulants to albumin.

CRYSTALLINE STRUCTURES OF COMPLEXES AND THERMODYNAMIC TREATMENT OF STABILITY CONSTANTS

Crystalline Structures of Complexes

Crystalline structures of complexes provide detailed information about the arrangement of atoms within a molecule, which is crucial for understanding the nature and properties of complexation. Techniques like X-ray crystallography and neutron diffraction are commonly used to determine these structures.

1. **X-ray Crystallography:**
   a. **Principle**: This technique involves directing X-rays at a crystal and analyzing the diffraction pattern to determine the electron density and, subsequently, the atomic structure of the complex.
   b. **Application:** Used to elucidate the 3D structure of metal-ligand complexes, protein-ligand complexes, and other crystalline substances.
   c. **Example**: The structure of hemoglobin, which revealed the arrangement of iron within the heme group and how it binds to oxygen.
   d. **Impact:** Provides high-resolution structural information that is essential for understanding the molecular geometry, bonding interactions, and functional mechanisms of complexes.

2. **Neutron Diffraction:**
   a. **Principle:** Similar to X-ray crystallography but uses neutrons instead of X-rays. This technique is particularly useful for locating light atoms like hydrogen in a complex.
   b. **Application:** Studying the detailed hydrogen bonding networks and positions of light atoms in metal-organic frameworks and biological macromolecules.
   c. **Example:** Determining the hydrogen positions in enzyme-substrate complexes to understand catalytic mechanisms.
   d. **Impact:** Complements X-ray crystallography by providing additional information about hydrogen positions and isotopic compositions.

Thermodynamic Treatment of Stability Constants

The stability of complexes is quantified by stability constants (also known as formation constants), which are equilibrium constants for the formation of a complex from its components. Thermodynamic treatment of these constants provides insights into the strength and nature of interactions within the complex.

1. **Stability Constants (K):**
   a. **Definition**: The equilibrium constant for the formation of a complex from its constituent ions or molecules. It is expressed as:

   $$K=[ML][M][L]$$

2. **Where:**
   a. $[ML]$ is the concentration of the complex, $[M]$ is the concentration of the free metal ion, and $[L]$ is the concentration of the free ligand.
   b. **Significance:** A higher stability constant indicates a more stable complex.

3. **Stepwise Formation Constants:**
   a. **Definition**: These constants describe the sequential addition of ligands to a metal ion, forming intermediate species.
   b. **Example**: For the formation of a complex MLn through sequential steps, the stepwise constants are given by:

   $$K1=[ML][M][L]$$

   $$K2=[ML2][ML][L]$$

   Significance: Stepwise constants provide a detailed understanding of the complexation process, indicating the stability of each intermediate species.

4. **Cumulative Formation Constants (β):**
   a. **Definition**: The overall equilibrium constant for the formation of a complex from the free metal ion and free ligands.
   b. **Example**: For a complex MLn, the cumulative formation constant is:

   $$\beta n=[MLn][M][L]n$$

   c. **Significance**: Provides a comprehensive measure of the stability of the complex.

5. **Thermodynamic Parameters:**
   Gibbs Free Energy (ΔG):

   $$\Delta G=-RT\ln K$$

6. **Where:**
   a. R is the gas constant and
   b. T is the temperature in Kelvin.

   > **Significance**: A negative ΔG indicates a spontaneous formation of the complex.

   c. **Enthalpy (ΔH):**
      i. **Measurement**: Determined through calorimetric methods or van't Hoff analysis.
      ii. **Significance**: Provides insights into the heat changes during complex formation, indicating whether the process is endothermic or exothermic.
   d. Entropy (ΔS):

$$\Delta G = \Delta H - T\Delta S$$

      i. **Significance:** Reflects the degree of disorder or randomness associated with the formation of the complex.

Analytical Methods for Determining Stability Constants

1. **Potentiometry:**
   a. **Principle:** Measures the potential of a solution to determine the concentration of free ions, which can be used to calculate stability constants.
   b. **Application**: Used for metal-ligand complexes in solution.
   c. **Example**: Titration of a metal ion with a ligand and monitoring the pH to determine the formation constant.
   d. **Impact:** Provides accurate and quantitative data on complex stability.

2. **Spectrophotometry:**
   a. **Principle**: Measures the absorbance or emission of light by the complex to determine concentrations.
   b. **Application**: Suitable for colored complexes or those with distinct absorption/emission spectra.

c. **Example**: Determining the stability constant of a metal-porphyrin complex by analyzing its UV-Vis absorbance.

d. **Impact:** Allows for the monitoring of complex formation in real-time and under various conditions.

3. **Calorimetry:**

   a. **Principle**: Measures the heat change associated with complex formation to derive thermodynamic parameters.

   b. **Application**: Isothermal titration calorimetry (ITC) directly measures the heat released or absorbed during complexation.

   c. **Example**: Studying the binding of small molecules to proteins by measuring the heat of interaction.

   d. **Impact:** Provides direct measurements of ΔH and ΔS, offering comprehensive thermodynamic profiles.

4. **NMR Spectroscopy:**

   a. **Principle:** Observes the magnetic properties of nuclei in the complex to determine binding interactions and dynamics.

   b. **Application**: Suitable for studying both small and large complexes in solution.

   c. **Example**: Using 1H NMR to determine the binding constant of a ligand to a metal ion.

   d. **Impact:** Offers detailed structural and dynamic information about the complex in solution.

5. **Electrochemical Methods:**

   a. **Principle:** Measures the electrochemical properties of complexes, such as redox potentials.

   b. **Application**: Cyclic voltammetry can be used to study the formation and stability of redox-active complexes.

   c. **Example**: Analyzing the redox behavior of metal complexes with organic ligands.

d. **Impact:** Provides insights into the redox stability and electron transfer properties of complexes.

Multiple-Choice Questions (MCQs)

1. What type of bond characterizes coordination complexes?

    A) Ionic

    B) Covalent

    C) Coordinate covalent

    D) Hydrogen

2. Which method is used to measure the heat released or absorbed during a binding reaction?

    A) Surface Plasmon Resonance (SPR)

    B) Isothermal Titration Calorimetry (ITC)

    C) X-ray Crystallography

    D) Mass Spectrometry (MS)

3. What is the role of cyclodextrins in drug delivery?

    A) Increase drug bioactivity

    B) Enhance drug solubility

    C) Decrease drug absorption

    D) Reduce drug stability

4. Which complexation is associated with the binding of oxygen to hemoglobin?

    A) Irreversible binding

    B) Reversible binding

    C) Covalent binding

    D) Non-covalent binding

5. What type of interaction is primarily involved in hydrogen-bonded complexes?

    A) Ionic

B) Van der Waals

C) Covalent

D) Hydrogen bonding

6. Which spectroscopy technique involves the differential absorption of left and right circularly polarized light?

    A) UV-Visible Spectroscopy

    B) Fluorescence Spectroscopy

    C) Circular Dichroism (CD) Spectroscopy

    D) NMR Spectroscopy

7. Which of the following is a characteristic of homogeneous catalysis?

    A) Catalyst and reactants in different phases

    B) Utilizes solid catalysts in liquid phase

    C) Catalyst and reactants in the same phase

    D) Only uses gaseous reactants

8. What describes the lock and key model of protein binding?

    A) Ligand induces a change in protein shape upon binding.

    B) Protein and ligand do not change shapes upon binding.

    C) Binding involves multiple protein and ligand conformations.

    D) Protein binds multiple ligands simultaneously.

9. What is the principle of molecular docking?

    A) Measures refractive index changes due to protein-ligand interactions.

    B) Predicts the preferred binding modes of ligands to protein targets.

    C) Uses heat measurement to analyze protein-ligand interactions.

    D) Detects fluorescence emitted by protein-ligand complexes.

10. What is the role of EDTA in chelation therapy?

    A) To increase heavy metal absorption

    B) To stabilize heavy metal compounds

    C) To facilitate the excretion of heavy metals

    D) To reduce the solubility of heavy metals

11. Which type of ligands donates multiple electron pairs to the central atom/ion?

    A) Monodentate

    B) Bidentate

    C) Polydentate

    D) Aliphatic

12. What is significant about the stability constant (K) of a complex?

    A) A higher K indicates a less stable complex.

    B) It is only applicable to organic complexes.

    C) A higher K indicates a more stable complex.

    D) It decreases with increasing ligand concentration.

13. Which term describes ligands that can form more than two coordinate bonds with a central atom?

    A) Monodentate

    B) Bidentate

    C) Polydentate

    D) Non-dentate

14. What does the induced fit model explain about protein binding?

    A) Proteins have rigid structures that do not change upon ligand binding.

    B) Ligand binding does not induce changes in protein or ligand structure.

    C) Ligand binding induces a conformational change in the protein for a tighter fit.

    D) Proteins pre-exist in multiple conformations before ligand binding.

15. In which type of catalysis are the reactants and catalysts in different phases?

    A) Homogeneous catalysis

    B) Heterogeneous catalysis

    C) Bio-catalysis

    D) Auto-catalysis

16. What is the primary application of X-ray crystallography?

A) To measure the concentration of metal ions in solution

B) To determine the three-dimensional structure of complexes

C) To evaluate the stability of complexes in various solvents

D) To measure the absorption spectra of metal complexes

17. Which spectroscopy technique is especially useful for studying the dynamics of complexes in solution?

A) UV-Visible Spectroscopy

B) X-ray Crystallography

C) NMR Spectroscopy

D) Circular Dichroism (CD) Spectroscopy

18. What is a primary use of metal-organic frameworks (MOFs)?

A) Increasing the reactivity of metal complexes

B) Catalyzing redox reactions only

C) Gas storage and separation

D) Solely for drug delivery

19. Which analytical technique provides real-time data on binding kinetics and affinity?

A) Mass Spectrometry

B) Isothermal Titration Calorimetry

C) Surface Plasmon Resonance

D) X-ray Crystallography

20. What role does protein binding play in pharmacokinetics?

A) It has no significant impact on drug distribution or metabolism.

B) It determines the drug's chemical stability and reactivity.

C) It affects the distribution, metabolism, and excretion of drugs.

D) It only affects the drug's solubility in bodily fluids.

Short Answer Type Questions (Subjective)

1. Define complexation and describe its significance in chemistry.

2. What is a coordination complex?

3. Explain the role of the central ion in complexation.

4. Describe the difference between monodentate and polydentate ligands.

5. How does temperature affect the stability of complexes?

6. What is the role of solvent in complexation reactions?

7. Explain the significance of the stability constant (K) in complexation.

8. What is chelation therapy and how does it utilize complexation?

9. How are coordination complexes used in catalysis?

10. Describe the structure of an inclusion complex and give an example.

11. What are ion pairs and how do they form?

12. How does the nature of the ligand affect complex stability?

13. Define reversible and irreversible protein binding.

14. What is the lock and key model of protein binding?

15. Explain the induced fit model and its significance.

16. How do environmental conditions like pH influence protein binding?

17. What is the role of protein binding in pharmacokinetics?

18. Describe the role of metal-organic frameworks (MOFs).

19. Explain how circular dichroism (CD) spectroscopy can be used to study protein-ligand interactions.

20. What are the applications of isothermal titration calorimetry (ITC) in studying complexation?

Long Answer Type Questions (Subjective)

1. Discuss the various types of complexes and their roles in biological systems and industrial applications.

2. Explain the factors that influence the stability and formation of complexes in chemical reactions.

3. Describe the various spectroscopic techniques used to analyze complexation and their specific applications.

4. Discuss the role of protein binding in drug design and how it influences the pharmacological activity of drugs.

5. Explain how metal complexes are used in environmental chemistry for pollutant removal and detection.

6. Provide a detailed account of the role of cyclodextrins in drug delivery systems, including mechanism and benefits.

7. Describe the role of protein-ligand interactions in enzyme catalysis, using a specific example to illustrate the mechanism.

8. Discuss the impact of protein binding on the distribution and metabolism of drugs in the human body.

9. Explain the principles and applications of surface plasmon resonance (SPR) in studying biomolecular interactions.

10. Provide a comprehensive overview of how complexation is utilized in sensing and detection technologies, with specific examples of chemosensors and luminescent probes.

Answer Key

1. C (Coordinate covalent)
2. B (Isothermal Titration Calorimetry)
3. B (Enhance drug solubility)
4. B (Reversible binding)
5. D (Hydrogen bonding)
6. C (Circular Dichroism (CD) Spectroscopy)
7. C (Catalyst and reactants in the same phase)
8. B (Protein and ligand do not change shapes upon binding.)
9. B (Predicts the preferred binding modes of ligands to protein targets.)
10. C (To facilitate the excretion of heavy metals)
11. C (Polydentate)
12. C (A higher K indicates a more stable complex.)

13.C (Polydentate)

14.C (Ligand binding induces a conformational change in the protein for a tighter fit.)

15.B (Heterogeneous catalysis)

16.B (To determine the three-dimensional structure of complexes)

17.C (NMR Spectroscopy)

18.C (Gas storage and separation)

19.C (Surface Plasmon Resonance)

20.C (It affects the distribution, metabolism, and excretion of drugs)

CHAPTER – 6

PH, BUFFERS AND ISOTONIC SOLUTIONS

INTRODUCTION:

pH:

pH is a measure of the acidity or basicity of a solution. It is defined as the negative logarithm of the concentration of hydrogen ions ($H+$) in a solution. The pH scale ranges from 0 to 14:

1. A pH less than 7 indicates acidity.

2. A pH of 7 indicates neutrality (where the concentration of $H+$ ions equals the concentration of hydroxide ($OH-$) ions).

3. A pH greater than 7 indicates alkalinity or basicity.

The pH scale is logarithmic, meaning that each whole pH value below 7 is ten times more acidic than the next higher value, and each whole pH value above 7 is ten times more alkaline than the next lower value.

Buffers:

Buffers are solutions that resist changes in pH when an acid or base is added to them. They are essential in biological systems, where maintaining a stable pH is crucial for various biochemical processes. Buffers typically consist of a weak acid and its conjugate base, or a weak base and its conjugate acid.

When an acid is added to a buffer solution, the weak base in the buffer reacts with the added acid, forming its conjugate acid, thus preventing a significant change in pH. Similarly, when a base is added, the weak acid in the buffer reacts with the added base to form its conjugate base, again preventing a significant change in pH.

Isotonic Solutions:

An isotonic solution refers to a solution that has the same concentration of solutes (particles) as another solution, typically referring to bodily fluids like blood or cell cytoplasm. In the context of physiology, isotonic solutions are crucial for maintaining proper cell function.

When a cell is placed in an isotonic solution, there is no net movement of water across the cell membrane because the concentration of solutes inside and outside the cell is the same. As a result, the cell maintains its shape and size.

In summary, pH, buffers, and isotonic solutions are all important concepts in chemistry and biology:

1. pH measures the acidity or basicity of a solution.
2. Buffers help maintain stable pH levels by resisting changes when acids or bases are added.
3. Isotonic solutions have the same concentration of solutes as bodily fluids, ensuring cells maintain their shape and size.

INTRODUCTION TO PH:

pH stands for "potential of hydrogen." It is a measure of the concentration of hydrogen ions ($H+$) in a solution. pH is a fundamental concept in chemistry, with broad applications in fields ranging from biology and environmental science to industry and medicine.

Historical Context:

The concept of pH was introduced by Danish chemist Søren Sørensen in 1909 as a means to simplify the expression of acidity and alkalinity. Initially, it was defined as the "hydrogen ion exponent." Later, the symbol pH was coined to represent this concept.

Definition:

pH is defined mathematically as the negative logarithm (base 10) of the hydrogen ion concentration:

$$pH = -\log_{10}[H+]$$

Where:

$[H+]$ represents the concentration of hydrogen ions in moles per liter (molarity).

The pH Scale:

The pH scale ranges from 0 to 14:

1. A pH less than 7 indicates acidity, with lower values indicating stronger acidity.
2. A pH of 7 is considered neutral, where the concentration of $H+$ions equals the concentration of hydroxide ions ($OH-$).
3. A pH greater than 7 indicates alkalinity or basicity, with higher values indicating stronger basicity.

Significance of pH:

pH plays a critical role in various chemical, biological, and environmental processes:

1. **Biological Systems**: pH is tightly regulated in living organisms. For instance, human blood pH is maintained within a narrow range (7.35 to 7.45) to support essential physiological functions.
2. **Chemical Reactions**: pH influences the rates and outcomes of chemical reactions. Many biochemical reactions in cells are sensitive to pH changes.
3. **Environmental Impact**: pH affects the health of ecosystems. Acid rain, for example, can lower the pH of soil and water bodies, leading to detrimental effects on plants, aquatic life, and infrastructure.
4. **Industrial Applications**: pH control is crucial in various industries, such as water treatment, food processing, and pharmaceutical manufacturing, to optimize processes and ensure product quality.

Measurement of pH:

pH can be measured using various methods, including pH meters, pH indicator papers, and pH probes. These tools allow for accurate determination of pH in different types of solutions, from aqueous solutions to biological fluids.

In summary, pH is a fundamental concept that quantifies the acidity or basicity of a solution. Its importance extends across diverse fields, making it a cornerstone of modern chemistry and biology.

INTRODUCTION OF BUFFERS

Buffers are solutions that resist changes in pH when an acid or base is added to them. They are vital in maintaining pH stability in various chemical, biological, and environmental processes. Buffers typically consist of a weak acid and its conjugate base, or a weak base and its conjugate acid.

How Buffers Work:

Buffers work through a process called buffering, which involves the reversible reaction between the weak acid and its conjugate base (or weak base and its conjugate acid) to counteract the effects of added acids or bases.

1. **Acidic Buffer Action:**
   a. When a strong acid is added to an acidic buffer, it reacts with the weak base component of the buffer, forming its conjugate acid.
   b. The formation of the conjugate acid consumes $H+$ ions, preventing a significant decrease in pH.

2. **Basic Buffer Action:**
   a. When a strong base is added to a basic buffer, it reacts with the weak acid component of the buffer, forming its conjugate base.
   b. The formation of the conjugate base consumes $OH-$ ions, preventing a significant increase in pH.

Importance of Buffers:

Buffers play several crucial roles in various fields:

1. **Biological Systems:**
   a. Biological fluids, such as blood and cytoplasm, rely on buffers to maintain stable pH levels necessary for proper cellular function.
   b. For example, the bicarbonate buffer system in blood helps regulate pH by balancing the levels of carbonic acid and bicarbonate ions.

2. **Laboratory Techniques:**

a. Buffers are essential in laboratory settings for maintaining constant pH conditions during experiments, particularly in biochemical assays and enzyme studies.

3. **Industrial Processes:**

   a. Many industrial processes require precise pH control to optimize chemical reactions and product quality. Buffers are employed to maintain stable pH conditions in these processes.

4. **Environmental Applications:**

   a. Buffers can help mitigate the effects of acid rain on ecosystems by neutralizing acidic pollutants in soil and water bodies.

Types of Buffers:

There are several types of buffers, including:

1. **Acetate Buffer**: Consists of acetic acid and sodium acetate.
2. **Phosphate Buffer**: Contains a mixture of dihydrogen phosphate and hydrogen phosphate ions.
3. **Tris Buffer**: Utilizes tris(hydroxymethyl)aminomethane and its conjugate acid.
4. **Good's Buffers**: Synthetic buffers designed for specific pH ranges and biological applications.

Buffer Capacity:

Buffer capacity refers to the ability of a buffer solution to resist changes in pH upon addition of an acid or base. Buffers with higher concentrations of the weak acid and its conjugate base (or weak base and its conjugate acid) have greater buffer capacity.

In summary, buffers are essential solutions that help maintain pH stability in various systems and processes. Their ability to resist pH changes makes them indispensable in fields ranging from biology and chemistry to industry and environmental science.

INTRODUCTION OF ISOTONIC SOLUTIONS

An isotonic solution refers to a solution that has the same concentration of solutes (particles) as another solution, typically referring to bodily fluids like blood or cell cytoplasm. In the context of physiology, isotonic solutions are crucial for maintaining proper cell function.

Characteristics of Isotonic Solutions:

1. **Equal Osmotic Pressure**: In an isotonic solution, the concentration of solutes is balanced both inside and outside the cell. This equilibrium ensures that there is no net movement of water across the cell membrane.

2. **Cellular Homeostasis**: Isotonic solutions help maintain the normal shape and volume of cells by preventing excessive water uptake or loss. Cells function optimally when they are in an environment with an isotonic osmolarity.

3. **Medical Applications**: Isotonic solutions are commonly used in medical settings for various purposes, including intravenous (IV) fluid therapy, wound irrigation, and medications.

Importance of Isotonic Solutions:

1. **Intravenous Fluids:**

    a. Isotonic saline (0.9% NaCl) is a common intravenous fluid used to replace lost fluids and electrolytes in patients with dehydration, shock, or certain medical conditions.

    b. Other isotonic solutions, such as Ringer's lactate and 5% dextrose in water (D5W), are also used depending on the specific needs of the patient.

2. **Cell Culture:**

    In cell culture techniques, maintaining cells in an isotonic environment is essential for their growth and viability. Isotonic cell culture media provide the necessary nutrients and osmotic balance for cells to thrive.

3. **Ophthalmic Solutions:**

   Isotonic saline and other isotonic solutions are used in ophthalmology for procedures such as eye irrigation, contact lens cleaning, and eye drops.

4. **Pharmaceutical Formulations:**

   Isotonic solutions are incorporated into pharmaceutical formulations to ensure compatibility with biological tissues and minimize irritation upon administration.

Hypertonic and Hypotonic Solutions:

a. **Hypertonic Solution**: A solution with a higher concentration of solutes compared to another solution. When a cell is placed in a hypertonic solution, water flows out of the cell, causing it to shrink or undergo crenation.

b. **Hypotonic Solution**: A solution with a lower concentration of solutes compared to another solution. When a cell is placed in a hypotonic solution, water flows into the cell, causing it to swell or undergo lysis (bursting).

Isotonicity in Relation to pH and Buffers:

a. Isotonic solutions, while primarily concerned with osmotic balance, can also have specific pH levels and may contain buffer components to maintain pH stability, especially in biological and medical applications.

b. The pH of an isotonic solution may vary depending on its composition and intended use. Buffers may be added to isotonic solutions to prevent significant changes in pH when exposed to acids or bases.

SORENSEN'S PH SCALE

Sørensen's pH scale, introduced by Danish chemist Søren Sørensen in 1909, is a logarithmic scale used to measure the acidity or basicity of a solution. It serves as the foundation for modern pH measurement and provides a standardized method for quantifying the concentration of hydrogen ions ($H+$) in a solution.

Sørensen's pH Scale:

Definition:

Sørensen defined pH as the negative logarithm (base 10) of the hydrogen ion concentration:

$$pH = -\log_{10}[H+]$$

Where:

[H+] represents the concentration of hydrogen ions in moles per liter (molarity).

Characteristics:

1. **Logarithmic Scale:** The pH scale is logarithmic, meaning that each unit change in pH represents a tenfold change in hydrogen ion concentration. For example, a solution with a pH of 5 is ten times more acidic than a solution with a pH of 6.

2. **Range:** Sørensen's pH scale ranges from 0 to 14:
   a. pH values less than 7 indicate acidity, with lower values representing stronger acidity.
   b. A pH of 7 is considered neutral, where the concentration of $H+$ ions equals the concentration of hydroxide ions ($OH-$).
   c. pH values greater than 7 indicate alkalinity, with higher values representing stronger alkalinity.
   c. **Standardization:** Sørensen's pH scale provides a standardized method for comparing acidity and basicity across different solutions, making it a widely accepted tool in chemistry, biology, and various industries.

Application in pH Measurement:

Sørensen's pH scale forms the basis for pH measurement techniques used in laboratories and industries worldwide. Various methods are employed to measure pH accurately, including pH meters, pH indicator papers, and pH probes. These tools utilize Sørensen's scale to quantify the acidity or basicity of a solution based on the concentration of $H+$ ions.

Connection to Buffers and Isotonic Solutions:

1. **Buffers:** Sørensen's pH scale is essential for characterizing the effectiveness of buffer solutions in maintaining pH stability. Buffers are designed to resist changes in pH upon addition of acids or bases, and their performance is evaluated based on their ability to maintain pH within a desired range on Sørensen's scale.

2. **Isotonic Solutions**: While Sørensen's pH scale primarily quantifies acidity and basicity, isotonic solutions may have specific pH levels within this scale. Isotonicity refers to osmotic balance rather than pH, but pH stability may be important in certain isotonic solutions used in biological and medical applications. Buffers may be incorporated into isotonic solutions to maintain pH within a physiological range compatible with living tissues.

PH DETERMINATION BY ELECTROMETRIC

pH determination by electrometric methods is a widely used technique in chemistry, biology, environmental science, and various industries. Electrometric methods rely on measuring the electrical potential difference (voltage) between a reference electrode and a glass electrode sensitive to hydrogen ion concentration $(H+)$. This approach allows for accurate and precise determination of pH in solutions.

Principle of Electrometric pH Determination:

1. **Glass Electrode**: The key component in electrometric pH determination is the glass electrode. It consists of a thin glass membrane that is sensitive to hydrogen ions $(H+)$. The glass membrane is typically composed of special glass containing metal ions (usually lithium, sodium, or potassium) that exchange with hydrogen ions in the solution being measured.

2. **Reference Electrode**: In addition to the glass electrode, a reference electrode is used to provide a stable reference potential against which the potential of the glass electrode is measured. The reference electrode is usually a calomel electrode or a silver/silver chloride electrode.

3. **Nernst Equation**: The potential difference measured by the glass electrode is related to the pH of the solution according to the Nernst equation:

$$E = E0 + 0.059 n \log f_0 [H+]$$

Where:

E is the measured potential.

$E0$ is the standard electrode potential.

n is the number of electrons involved in the reaction (usually 1 for pH electrodes).

$[H+]$ is the concentration of hydrogen ions.

Procedure for ph determination:

1. **Calibration**: Before use, the pH meter must be calibrated using standard buffer solutions of known pH values. This ensures accurate measurements across the pH range of interest.

2. **Sample measurement**: Once calibrated, the glass electrode is immersed in the solution whose pH is to be determined. The reference electrode is also immersed in the same solution. The potential difference between the glass and reference electrodes is measured by the pH meter and converted into pH units.

3. **Temperature correction**: pH measurements are often temperature-dependent. Some pH meters include automatic temperature compensation (ATC) to correct for temperature variations and ensure accurate pH readings.

Advantages of electrometric ph determination:

a. **Accuracy**: Electrometric methods offer high accuracy in pH determination, especially when calibrated properly and used with high-quality electrodes.

b. **PrecisioN:** These methods provide precise measurements, making them suitable for both research and industrial applications.

c. **Wide range**: Electrometric pH meters can measure pH over a wide range, from highly acidic to highly alkaline solutions.

d. **Speed**: pH determination using electrometric methods is relatively quick, allowing for rapid analysis of samples.

Applications:

a. **Laboratory research**: Electrometric pH determination is widely used in chemical laboratories for research, quality control, and analytical testing.

b. **Industrial processes**: pH measurement is essential in various industrial processes, including water treatment, food and beverage production, pharmaceutical manufacturing, and chemical synthesis.

c. **Environmental monitoring**: pH measurement plays a crucial role in environmental monitoring of water bodies, soil, and atmospheric samples.

PH DETERMINATION BY CALORIMETRIC

pH determination by colorimetric methods is another common technique used to measure the acidity or basicity of a solution. Colorimetric methods rely on the use of pH indicators, which are substances that change color in response to changes in pH. These methods are often simpler and more cost-effective than electrometric methods, making them suitable for various applications.

Principle of Colorimetric pH Determination:

1. **pH Indicators**: pH indicators are typically weak acids or bases that undergo a reversible color change as the pH of the solution changes. The color change occurs due to protonation or deprotonation of the indicator molecule, leading to different absorption spectra for the protonated and deprotonated forms.

2. **Absorption Spectra**: Each pH indicator has a characteristic absorption spectrum, with distinct colors corresponding to different pH ranges. By measuring the intensity of light absorbed by the solution at specific wavelengths, the pH of the solution can be determined.

3. **Calibration**: Before use, the pH indicator must be calibrated using standard buffer solutions of known pH values. This allows for the establishment of a calibration curve relating the observed color change to the pH of the solution.

Procedure for pH Determination:

1. **Selection of pH Indicator**: Choose a pH indicator suitable for the pH range of the solution being measured. Different indicators have different pH ranges over which they change color.

2. **Preparation of Sample**: Prepare the sample solution whose pH is to be determined. Ensure that the solution is clear and free of any interfering substances that could affect the colorimetric measurement.

3. **Addition of Indicator**: Add a small amount of pH indicator to the sample solution. The indicator will change color based on the pH of the solution.

4. **Observation of Color Change**: Observe the color change in the solution and compare it to a color chart or colorimeter calibration curve to determine the pH of the solution.

Advantages of Colorimetric pH Determination:

a. **Simplicity**: Colorimetric methods are simple and easy to use, requiring minimal equipment and expertise.

b. **Cost-Effectiveness**: These methods are often more cost-effective than electrometric methods, making them suitable for routine analysis and field applications.

c. **Rapid Analysis**: Colorimetric pH determination can provide rapid results, allowing for high-throughput analysis of samples.

Limitations:

a. **Limited pH Range**: pH indicators have specific pH ranges over which they change color effectively. Care must be taken to select the appropriate indicator for the pH range of the solution being measured.

b. **Subjectivity**: Interpretation of color changes can be subjective, particularly when comparing to color charts. The use of colorimeters can help overcome this limitation by providing objective measurements of color intensity.

Applications:

a. **Educational Demonstrations**: Colorimetric pH determination is often used in educational settings to demonstrate principles of acid-base chemistry.

b. **Environmental Monitoring**: These methods are used for rapid assessment of pH in environmental samples, such as water and soil.

c. **Clinical Diagnostics**: Colorimetric pH determination is utilized in clinical laboratories for analyzing bodily fluids and diagnostic tests.

Applications Of Buffers

Buffers play essential roles in various fields due to their ability to maintain stable pH levels in solutions. Here are some detailed applications of buffers:

1. Biological and Biochemical Systems:

a. **Cellular Physiology**: Biological systems, such as cells and tissues, require tightly regulated pH levels for proper functioning. Buffers, such as the phosphate buffer system and the bicarbonate buffer system, play critical roles in maintaining the pH of intracellular and extracellular fluids within narrow physiological ranges.

b. **Enzyme Catalysis:** Many enzymes exhibit optimal activity at specific pH levels. Buffers help maintain the pH of enzyme reaction mixtures, ensuring optimal catalytic activity and stability. For example, the Tris-HCl buffer is commonly used in biochemical assays to maintain pH stability.

2. Laboratory Techniques:

a. **Biochemical Assays**: Buffers are used in biochemical assays to maintain constant pH conditions, ensuring reproducible and reliable results. Buffer selection depends on the desired pH range and compatibility with assay components.

b. **Electrophoresis**: Buffers are crucial in gel electrophoresis techniques for separating biomolecules, such as DNA, RNA, and proteins. Tris-acetate and Tris-borate buffers are commonly used in nucleic acid electrophoresis, while Tris-glycine buffer is preferred for protein electrophoresis.

3. Pharmaceutical and Biotechnological Applications:

a. **Drug Formulations**: Buffers are incorporated into pharmaceutical formulations to maintain the stability and efficacy of drugs. Buffer systems are carefully selected to ensure compatibility with drug molecules and physiological conditions.

b. **Bioprocessing**: Buffers are used in biotechnological processes, such as fermentation and protein purification, to maintain optimal pH conditions for microbial growth and protein stability. Common buffers in bioprocessing include phosphate, acetate, and citrate buffers.

4. Analytical Chemistry:

a. **pH Measurement**: Buffers are used as reference solutions for calibrating pH meters and electrodes in analytical chemistry. Standard buffer solutions of known pH values allow for accurate pH measurements in samples of interest.

b. **Titration**: Buffers are employed in acid-base titrations to resist changes in pH and maintain the equivalence point. This ensures accurate determination of the unknown concentration of an analyte.

5. Environmental Monitoring:

a. **Water Treatment**: Buffers play a role in water treatment processes, such as wastewater treatment and potable water purification. Buffering agents help stabilize pH levels in water bodies, preventing fluctuations that can harm aquatic ecosystems.

b. **Soil Remediation**: Buffers are utilized in soil remediation efforts to neutralize acidic or alkaline soils and restore pH balance. Buffering agents aid in maintaining optimal conditions for plant growth and microbial activity.

In summary, buffers have diverse applications in biological, biochemical, pharmaceutical, environmental, and analytical settings. Their ability to maintain stable pH levels makes them indispensable in a wide range of scientific and industrial processes.

BUFFER EQUATION

The buffer equation describes the relationship between the pH of a buffer solution, the pKa (acid dissociation constant) of the weak acid component of the buffer, and the concentrations of the weak acid ($[HA]$) and its conjugate base ($[A-]$). This equation is fundamental to understanding how buffers function to resist changes in pH when acids or bases are added to the solution.

Buffer Equation:

The Henderson-Hasselbalch equation is commonly used to represent the buffer equation:

$$pH = pKa + \log_{10}([A-][HA])$$

Where:

pH is the pH of the buffer solution.

pKa is the negative logarithm (base 10) of the acid dissociation constant (Ka) of the weak acid.

$[A-]$ is the concentration of the conjugate base of the weak acid.

$[HA]$ is the concentration of the weak acid.

Understanding the Buffer Equation:

1. **pH and pKa Relationship:**

    a. The term pKa represents the pH at which the weak acid (HA) is 50% dissociated into its conjugate base ($A-$) and hydrogen ions ($H+$). It serves as a measure of the acid's strength.

    b. When the pH of the buffer solution equals the pKa of the weak acid, the concentrations of HA and $A-$are equal, resulting in a pH equal to the pKa.

2. **Buffer Capacity:**

    a. The buffer capacity is maximized when the concentrations of HA and $A-$are roughly equal. This occurs when the pH of the buffer solution is close to the pKa of the weak acid.

    b. Buffers with higher concentrations of both

    c. HA and $A-$have greater buffer capacity and can resist changes in pH more effectively.

3. **Effect of Adding Acid or Base:**

    a. When a small amount of acid or base is added to a buffer solution, the buffer equation predicts the resulting change in pH.

    b. If an acid is added, the equilibrium shifts to consume the added $H+$ions, primarily by converting $A-$ to HA, resulting in a minimal change in pH.

    c. If a base is added, the equilibrium shifts to consume the added $OH-$ions, primarily by converting HA to $A-$, again resulting in a minimal change in pH.

Applications of the Buffer Equation:

1. **Buffer Design**: The buffer equation guides the selection of appropriate buffer systems for specific pH ranges and applications. It helps ensure that buffers maintain stable pH levels under varying conditions.

2. **Biological and Biochemical Studies**: The buffer equation is used to design buffers for maintaining physiological pH ranges in biological and biochemical experiments, such as enzyme assays and cell culture.

3. **Analytical Chemistry**: In analytical chemistry, the buffer equation is utilized to prepare standard buffer solutions for calibrating pH meters and electrodes, as well as for controlling pH in titration experiments.

4. **Industrial Processes**: The buffer equation informs the design of buffer systems for controlling pH in industrial processes, such as water treatment, food production, and pharmaceutical manufacturing.

BUFFER CAPACITY

Buffer capacity is a measure of the ability of a buffer solution to resist changes in pH when acids or bases are added. It quantifies the effectiveness of a buffer in maintaining pH stability and is crucial in various chemical, biological, and industrial processes.

Buffer Capacity Equation:

The buffer capacity (β) of a buffer solution can be defined in terms of the change in the concentration of the acid or base component ($\Delta[HA]$) divided by the corresponding change in pH (ΔpH):

$$\beta = \Delta[HA]\Delta\text{pH}$$

Understanding Buffer Capacity:

1. **High Buffer Capacity:**
   a. Buffers with high buffer capacity can resist changes in pH even when relatively large amounts of acid or base are added.
   b. Buffer capacity is maximized when the concentrations of the weak acid (HA) and its conjugate base ($A-$) are roughly equal.

2. **pH Range:**
   a. Buffer capacity is highest at pH values close to the pKa of the weak acid component of the buffer.

   b. As the pH moves away from the pKa, the buffer capacity decreases, making the buffer less effective at resisting changes in pH.

3. **Buffer Composition:**

   a. Buffer capacity depends on the concentrations of HA and A^- in the buffer solution. Higher concentrations of both components result in higher buffer capacity.

   b. Buffers with a greater concentration of the weak acid or base have higher buffer capacity.

4. **Effect of Buffer Volume:**

   a. Increasing the volume of a buffer solution increases its buffer capacity because there is more buffer material available to resist changes in pH.

5. **Effect of Dilution:**

   a. Diluting a buffer solution decreases its buffer capacity because the concentrations of HA and A^- decrease, reducing the ability of the buffer to resist changes in pH.

Applications of Buffer Capacity:

1. **Biological Systems:**

   a. Buffer capacity is critical for maintaining stable pH levels in biological systems, such as blood, intracellular fluids, and cell culture media.

   b. Biological buffers, such as the phosphate buffer system and the bicarbonate buffer system, help regulate pH in physiological environments.

2. **Laboratory Techniques:**

   a. Buffer capacity is important in laboratory experiments where precise control of pH is necessary, such as enzyme assays, nucleic acid hybridization, and protein purification.

3. **Industrial Processes:**
    a. Buffer capacity is essential in various industrial processes, including food and beverage production, pharmaceutical manufacturing, and wastewater treatment.
    b. Buffer solutions are used to control pH during chemical reactions, product formulations, and environmental remediation processes.

4. **Analytical Chemistry:**
    a. Buffer capacity influences the accuracy and precision of pH measurements in analytical chemistry techniques, such as titrations, spectroscopy, and chromatography.

5. **Medical Applications:**
    a. Buffer capacity is important in medical diagnostics and drug formulations, where maintaining physiological pH ranges is critical for patient health and medication efficacy.

BUFFERS IN PHARMACEUTICAL

Buffers play crucial roles in pharmaceutical formulations, ensuring the stability, efficacy, and safety of medications. Here's a detailed look at the use of buffers in the pharmaceutical industry:

1. Stability of Active Ingredients:

a. **pH Control**: Many active pharmaceutical ingredients (APIs) are sensitive to changes in pH. Buffers are added to pharmaceutical formulations to maintain the desired pH range, thereby enhancing the stability of APIs.

b. **Prevention of Degradation**: Buffers help prevent chemical degradation of APIs by maintaining pH levels that minimize hydrolysis, oxidation, and other degradation pathways.

c. **Compatibility**: Buffers are selected based on their compatibility with both the API and other excipients in the formulation to ensure stability throughout the product's shelf life.

2. Oral Formulations:

a. **Gastrointestinal Stability**: Oral medications encounter varying pH conditions in the gastrointestinal tract. Buffers are incorporated into oral formulations to ensure that the drug remains stable and bioavailable in acidic stomach environments and alkaline intestinal environments.

b. **Taste Masking**: Some APIs have unpleasant tastes or cause irritation. Buffers can be used to adjust the pH of oral formulations to improve taste and reduce irritation upon administration.

3. Parenteral Formulations:

a. **Injectable Solutions**: Buffers are essential in injectable formulations, such as solutions for intravenous (IV) administration or injections. They help maintain the pH of the solution within a physiologically compatible range to minimize tissue irritation and ensure the stability of the drug.

b. **Compatibility with Biological Fluids**: Injectable medications must be compatible with biological fluids, such as blood and plasma. Buffers ensure that the pH of the formulation matches the pH of the target biological fluid, optimizing drug delivery and minimizing adverse effects.

4. Topical Formulations:

a. **Skin Compatibility**: Topical medications, such as creams, gels, and ointments, often require specific pH ranges to ensure compatibility with the skin. Buffers help maintain the pH of topical formulations to minimize irritation and enhance drug penetration.

b. **Preservation**: Buffers can also contribute to the preservation of topical formulations by controlling pH, which can affect the growth of microorganisms and the stability of preservatives.

5. Ophthalmic Formulations:

a. **Eye Compatibility**: Ophthalmic medications, such as eye drops and ointments, must be compatible with the pH of ocular tissues to avoid irritation or damage. Buffers are used to adjust the pH of ophthalmic formulations to match the pH of tears and ensure safety and efficacy.

b. **Sterility**: Buffers contribute to the maintenance of sterility in ophthalmic formulations by controlling pH, which can affect the growth of microorganisms and the efficacy of preservatives.

6. Inhalation Formulations:

a. **Respiratory Compatibility**: Inhalation medications, such as aerosols and inhalers, require specific pH ranges to ensure compatibility with the respiratory tract. Buffers help maintain the pH of inhalation formulations to minimize irritation and ensure drug delivery to the target site.

b. **Stability of Aerosols**: Buffers play a role in stabilizing aerosol formulations, ensuring that the suspended particles or droplets remain dispersed and do not aggregate or settle out of the formulation.

BUFFERS IN BIOLOGICAL SYSTEMS

Buffers play critical roles in biological systems, maintaining stable pH levels essential for cellular functions, enzyme activities, and physiological processes. Here's an in-depth look at the significance of buffers in biological systems:

Intracellular pH Regulation:

Intracellular pH regulation is a vital process in maintaining cellular homeostasis and ensuring proper cellular function. Buffers play a crucial role in this regulation within biological systems. Here's a detailed exploration:

1. Importance of Intracellular pH Regulation:

a. **Cellular Homeostasis**: Intracellular pH regulation is essential for maintaining cellular homeostasis, as many biochemical reactions are pH-dependent. Proper pH levels are necessary for enzyme activity, protein structure, and ion transport across cell membranes.

b. **Cellular Signaling**: Intracellular pH plays a role in cellular signaling pathways, influencing processes such as cell growth, differentiation, and apoptosis. Changes in pH can modulate the activity of signaling molecules and affect cellular responses to stimuli.

2. Buffers in Intracellular pH Regulation:

a. **Intracellular Buffers**: Cells contain various buffering systems to regulate intracellular pH. These include proteins with ionizable side chains (e.g., histidine residues), organic phosphate compounds, and bicarbonate/carbonic acid (HCO_3^-/H_2CO_3) systems.

b. **Protein Buffering**: Proteins act as intracellular buffers by accepting or donating protons to maintain pH equilibrium. Many proteins have ionizable amino acid residues (e.g., histidine, lysine, arginine) that can serve as buffering sites.

c. **Phosphate Buffer System**: The phosphate buffer system, involving the dissociation of $H_2PO_4^-$ and HPO_4^{2-} ions, helps regulate intracellular pH. Phosphate compounds in the cell can act as buffering agents, particularly in acidic cellular environments.

3. **Mechanisms of Intracellular pH Regulation:**

a. **Proton Pumps**: Cells use membrane-bound proton pumps, such as the Na^+/H^+ exchanger (NHE) and the vacuolar H^+-ATPase (V-ATPase), to actively transport protons across cell membranes, regulating intracellular pH.

b. **Bicarbonate Transporters**: Bicarbonate ions (HCO_3^-) are transported across cell membranes by specific transporters, such as the sodium-bicarbonate cotransporter (NBC) and the chloride-bicarbonate exchanger (AE), contributing to intracellular pH regulation.

c. **Carbonic Anhydrase**: Carbonic anhydrase enzymes catalyze the interconversion between carbon dioxide (CO_2) and bicarbonate ions (HCO_3^-) within cells, facilitating pH regulation by modulating the concentration of these species.

4. **Role in Cellular Function:**

a. **Enzyme Activity: Intracellular** pH influences the activity of enzymes, with each enzyme having an optimal pH range for activity. pH deviations from the optimum can affect enzyme kinetics and metabolic pathways.

b. **Ion Transport**: Intracellular pH affects the activity of ion channels and transporters, influencing the movement of ions (e.g., Na^+, K^+, Ca^{2+}) across cell membranes. pH changes can alter membrane potential and cellular excitability.

c. **Protein Structure**: pH fluctuations can disrupt protein structure and function by affecting protein folding, stability, and interactions. Maintaining intracellular pH within a narrow range is crucial for preserving protein integrity.

5. Implications in Disease:

a. **Acid-Base Disorders**: Dysregulation of intracellular pH can contribute to acid-base disorders such as acidosis or alkalosis, which have implications for cellular function, metabolism, and disease pathogenesis.

b. **Cancer Metabolism**: Altered intracellular pH regulation is a hallmark of cancer cells and is associated with tumor growth, invasion, and metastasis. Targeting pH regulatory mechanisms is a potential therapeutic strategy in cancer treatment.

Blood pH Regulation:

Blood pH regulation is a critical physiological process necessary for maintaining homeostasis and ensuring the proper function of various bodily systems. Buffers in biological systems, particularly within the blood, play a crucial role in regulating pH levels. Here's a detailed exploration:

1. Importance of Blood pH Regulation:

a. **Acid-Base Balance**: Blood pH regulation is essential for maintaining the body's acid-base balance, ensuring that the pH of arterial blood remains within a narrow physiological range. The normal blood pH range is approximately 7.35 to 7.45.

b. **Enzyme Function**: Many enzymatic reactions in the body are pH-dependent. Proper blood pH levels are necessary for enzymes to maintain their optimal activity, facilitating essential metabolic processes.

c. **Cellular Function**: Blood pH influences cellular function and membrane permeability, affecting ion transport, protein structure, and cell signaling pathways. Deviations from normal pH levels can disrupt cellular homeostasis and function.

2. Buffers in Blood pH Regulation:

a. **Bicarbonate Buffer System**: The bicarbonate buffer system is the primary buffer system in the blood, involving the equilibrium between carbonic acid (H_2CO_3) and bicarbonate ions (HCO_3^-). This system plays a central role in maintaining blood pH stability.

b. **Hemoglobin Buffering**: Hemoglobin, the oxygen-carrying protein in red blood cells, can act as a buffer by binding to hydrogen ions (H^+) released during carbon dioxide (CO_2) transport and helping to maintain blood pH.

c. **Protein Buffering**: Plasma proteins, such as albumin and globulins, contain ionizable amino acid residues that can act as buffers, contributing to the overall buffering capacity of the blood.

3. Mechanisms of Blood pH Regulation:

a. **Respiratory Regulation**: The respiratory system regulates blood pH by controlling the elimination of carbon dioxide (CO_2) through respiration. Increased CO_2 levels lead to the formation of carbonic acid (H_2CO_3), lowering blood pH, while decreased CO_2 levels have the opposite effect.

b. **Renal Regulation**: The kidneys regulate blood pH by excreting hydrogen ions (H^+) and reabsorbing bicarbonate ions (HCO_3^-) into the bloodstream. This process helps maintain acid-base balance over the long term by adjusting the excretion of acidic or alkaline urine.

4. Role in Disease:

a. **Acid-Base Disorders**: Imbalances in blood pH, such as acidosis (low pH) or alkalosis (high pH), can occur due to various factors, including respiratory or metabolic disturbances. Acid-base disorders have implications for overall health and can affect organ function and cellular metabolism.

b. **Respiratory Acidosis/Alkalosis**: Respiratory disorders, such as hypoventilation (respiratory acidosis) or hyperventilation (respiratory alkalosis), can lead to changes in blood pH by altering CO_2 levels and carbonic acid concentrations.

c. **Metabolic Acidosis/Alkalosis**: Metabolic disorders, such as renal failure (metabolic acidosis) or excessive vomiting (metabolic alkalosis), can disrupt the body's acid-base balance by affecting the production or excretion of acids and bases.

5. Clinical Monitoring:

a. **Blood Gas Analysis**: Blood pH, along with other parameters such as pCO_2 (partial pressure of carbon dioxide) and bicarbonate levels, is routinely measured through blood gas analysis to assess acid-base status and guide clinical management in patients with respiratory or metabolic disorders.

b. **Buffering Capacity**: The buffering capacity of blood, determined by the concentrations of bicarbonate and other buffer components, provides insight into the blood's ability to resist changes in pH and maintain stability.

Buffering in Extracellular Fluids:

Buffering in extracellular fluids, such as interstitial fluid and plasma, is essential for maintaining pH homeostasis and ensuring proper physiological function. Here's a detailed exploration of buffering in extracellular fluids:

1. Importance of Buffering in Extracellular Fluids:

a. **pH Regulation**: Extracellular fluids play a crucial role in maintaining the overall pH balance of the body. Proper pH regulation is essential for enzymatic activity, protein function, and overall cellular metabolism.

b. **Ionic Balance**: Extracellular fluids help maintain the balance of ions, such as sodium (Na^+), potassium (K^+), calcium (Ca^{2+}), and chloride (Cl^-), which are vital for cellular function, nerve conduction, and muscle contraction.

2. Buffers in Extracellular Fluids:

a. **Bicarbonate Buffer System**: The bicarbonate buffer system is the primary buffering system in extracellular fluids. It involves the equilibrium between carbonic acid (H_2CO_3) and bicarbonate ions (HCO_3^-), which helps stabilize pH by accepting or releasing hydrogen ions (H^+) as needed.

b. **Protein Buffering**: Plasma proteins, such as albumin and globulins, contain ionizable amino acid residues that can act as buffers in extracellular fluids. These proteins help regulate pH by binding or releasing hydrogen ions based on environmental conditions.

c. **Other Buffer Systems**: Other buffer systems, such as phosphate buffers and ammonia/ammonium buffers, may also contribute to buffering in extracellular fluids, although to a lesser extent compared to the bicarbonate buffer system.

3. Mechanisms of Buffering in Extracellular Fluids:

a. **Respiratory Regulation**: The respiratory system contributes to pH regulation by controlling the elimination of carbon dioxide (CO_2) through respiration. Increased CO_2 levels lead to the formation of carbonic acid (H_2CO_3), lowering extracellular pH, while decreased CO_2 levels have the opposite effect.

b. **Renal Regulation**: The kidneys play a crucial role in pH regulation by selectively reabsorbing bicarbonate ions (HCO_3^-) and excreting hydrogen ions (H^+) into the urine. This renal mechanism helps maintain acid-base balance over the long term by adjusting the body's bicarbonate buffer capacity.

4. Clinical Implications:

   a. **Acid-Base Disorders**: Imbalances in extracellular pH, such as metabolic acidosis or alkalosis, can occur due to various factors, including renal dysfunction, respiratory disorders, or metabolic disturbances. These acid-base disorders have implications for overall health and may require medical intervention.

   b. **Diagnostic Testing**: Blood gas analysis is commonly used to assess extracellular pH and acid-base status in clinical settings. Measurement of parameters such as pH, partial pressure of carbon dioxide (pCO_2), and bicarbonate levels helps diagnose and monitor acid-base disorders.

5. Role in Health and Disease:

   a. **Maintaining Homeostasis**: Proper buffering in extracellular fluids is essential for maintaining physiological homeostasis and ensuring the proper function of organs and tissues throughout the body.

   b. **Disease Pathogenesis**: Dysregulation of extracellular pH can contribute to the pathogenesis of various diseases, including metabolic disorders, respiratory diseases, and renal dysfunction. Understanding the mechanisms of extracellular buffering is critical for elucidating disease mechanisms and developing targeted therapies.

4. Digestive System:

The digestive system employs various buffering mechanisms to maintain pH homeostasis throughout the gastrointestinal tract, ensuring optimal conditions for enzymatic activity, nutrient absorption, and overall digestive function. Here's a detailed exploration of buffering in the digestive system:

1. Importance of Buffering in the Digestive System:

   a. **pH Regulation**: Proper pH levels are essential for the functioning of digestive enzymes and the activation of specific digestive processes. Different regions of the gastrointestinal tract have varying pH requirements to facilitate digestion and nutrient absorption.

b. **Protection**: Buffering mechanisms in the digestive system help protect the mucosal lining of the gastrointestinal tract from damage caused by acidic or alkaline substances, digestive enzymes, and ingested irritants.

2. Buffering Mechanisms in the Digestive System:

a. **Salivary Buffering**: Saliva contains bicarbonate ions (HCO_3^-) and other buffering agents, such as phosphate ions, which help neutralize acidic substances and maintain a near-neutral pH in the oral cavity. This buffering action protects tooth enamel and facilitates the initial stages of digestion.

b. **Gastric Acid Secretion**: The stomach secretes hydrochloric acid (HCl) to aid in the digestion of proteins and activation of pepsinogen to pepsin. However, to prevent damage to the gastric mucosa, the stomach also secretes mucus and bicarbonate ions, forming a protective barrier and buffering the acidic environment.

c. **Pancreatic Secretions**: The pancreas secretes bicarbonate-rich pancreatic juice into the duodenum in response to the acidic chyme entering from the stomach. Bicarbonate ions neutralize gastric acid, raising the pH to a level suitable for pancreatic enzymes (e.g., pancreatic amylase, lipase, and proteases) to function optimally.

d. **Intestinal Secretions**: The small intestine also secretes bicarbonate-rich fluids, including bile from the liver and bicarbonate-rich pancreatic juice from the pancreas. These secretions help neutralize acidic chyme and maintain an alkaline pH in the small intestine, creating optimal conditions for enzymatic digestion and nutrient absorption.

3. Regulation of Gastric Acid Secretion:

a. **Gastric Acid Production**: Gastric acid (HCl) is produced by parietal cells in the gastric glands of the stomach. Acid secretion is stimulated by various factors, including histamine, acetylcholine, and gastrin, which activate specific receptors on parietal cells.

b. **Buffering by Mucus**: Mucus-secreting cells in the stomach produce a protective layer of mucus that covers the gastric mucosa, shielding it from the corrosive effects of gastric acid. Additionally, bicarbonate ions secreted by surface epithelial cells help buffer the acidic environment near the mucosal surface.

c. **Regulation by Prostaglandins**: Prostaglandins, such as prostaglandin E_2 (PGE_2), play a role in regulating gastric acid secretion and maintaining mucosal integrity. They stimulate mucus and bicarbonate secretion, promote blood flow to the gastric mucosa, and inhibit acid secretion.

4. Role in Digestive Disorders:

a. **Gastric Ulcers**: Disruption of the balance between acid secretion and mucosal defense mechanisms can lead to the development of gastric ulcers. Imbalances in gastric acid production, impaired mucosal barrier function, or infection with Helicobacter pylori can contribute to ulcer formation.

b. **Gastroesophageal Reflux Disease (GERD)**: GERD occurs when acidic gastric contents reflux into the esophagus, leading to symptoms such as heartburn, regurgitation, and esophageal inflammation. Altered gastric acid secretion and impaired esophageal sphincter function may contribute to GERD pathogenesis.

5. Clinical Considerations:

a. **Antacids**: Antacid medications, containing compounds such as aluminum hydroxide, magnesium hydroxide, or calcium carbonate, provide rapid relief from symptoms of acid indigestion and GERD by neutralizing gastric acid and raising gastric pH.

b. **Proton Pump Inhibitors (PPIs)**: PPIs, such as omeprazole and esomeprazole, are commonly used to reduce gastric acid secretion by inhibiting the proton pump (H^+/K^+ ATPase) on parietal cells. PPIs are effective in treating acid-related disorders, including GERD and peptic ulcers.

c. **H2-Receptor Antagonists**: H2-receptor antagonists, such as ranitidine and famotidine, block histamine receptors on parietal cells, reducing gastric acid secretion. These medications are used to treat acid-related disorders and provide symptom relief in conditions like GERD and peptic ulcers.

Buffering in Biological Fluids:

Buffering in biological fluids is a vital process that helps maintain pH homeostasis, ensuring optimal conditions for various biochemical reactions and physiological functions. Here's a detailed exploration of buffering in biological fluids:

1. Importance of Buffering in Biological Fluids:

a. **pH Regulation**: Biological fluids, such as blood, interstitial fluid, cytoplasm, and intracellular compartments, must maintain stable pH levels to support enzymatic activity, protein structure, and cellular metabolism.

b. **Cellular Function**: Proper pH levels are essential for cellular function, including membrane transport, enzyme kinetics, signal transduction, and protein-protein interactions. Deviations from optimal pH can disrupt these processes and lead to cellular dysfunction.

2. Buffering Systems in Biological Fluids:

a. **Bicarbonate Buffer System**: The bicarbonate buffer system is the primary buffering system in extracellular fluids, such as blood and interstitial fluid. It involves the equilibrium between carbonic acid (H_2CO_3) and bicarbonate ions (HCO_3^-), which helps stabilize pH by accepting or releasing hydrogen ions (H^+) as needed.

b. **Protein Buffering**: Proteins, both within cells and in extracellular fluids, contain ionizable amino acid residues (e.g., histidine, lysine) that can act as buffers. These proteins help regulate pH by binding or releasing hydrogen ions, depending on the surrounding pH.

c. **Phosphate Buffer System**: Phosphate ions ($HPO_4^{2-}/H_2PO_4^-$) serve as buffering agents, particularly in intracellular compartments such as the cytoplasm. Phosphate buffer systems help maintain pH stability within cells and organelles.

d. **Ammonia Buffer System**: Ammonia (NH_3) and ammonium ions (NH_4^+) can act as buffers, particularly in the renal tubules, where they play a role in acid-base regulation and ammonia excretion.

3. Mechanisms of Buffering in Biological Fluids:

a. **Respiratory Regulation**: The respiratory system regulates blood pH by controlling the elimination of carbon dioxide (CO_2) through respiration. Increased CO_2 levels lead to the formation of carbonic acid (H_2CO_3), lowering blood pH, while decreased CO_2 levels have the opposite effect.

b. **Renal Regulation**: The kidneys play a crucial role in pH regulation by selectively reabsorbing bicarbonate ions (HCO_3^-) and excreting hydrogen ions (H^+) into the urine. This renal mechanism helps maintain acid-base balance over the long term by adjusting the body's bicarbonate buffer capacity.

4. Clinical Considerations:

a. **Acid-Base Disorders**: Imbalances in pH, such as metabolic acidosis, metabolic alkalosis, respiratory acidosis, or respiratory alkalosis, can occur due to various factors, including renal dysfunction, respiratory disorders, or metabolic disturbances. These acid-base disorders have implications for overall health and may require medical intervention.

b. **Diagnostic Testing**: Blood gas analysis is commonly used to assess pH and acid-base status in clinical settings. Measurement of parameters such as pH, partial pressure of carbon dioxide (pCO_2), and bicarbonate levels helps diagnose and monitor acid-base disorders.

5. Therapeutic Interventions:

   a. **Medications:** Medications such as antacids, proton pump inhibitors (PPIs), and H2-receptor antagonists are used to treat acid-related disorders by altering gastric acid secretion or neutralizing gastric acid.

   b. **Fluid Replacement:** In cases of dehydration or electrolyte imbalances, intravenous fluids containing electrolytes (e.g., saline solutions) may be administered to restore fluid and pH balance.

Buffering in Cell Culture:

Buffering in cell culture is crucial for maintaining stable pH conditions within the growth medium, ensuring optimal conditions for cell viability, growth, and metabolism. Here's a detailed exploration of buffering in cell culture:

1. Importance of Buffering in Cell Culture:

   a. **Cell Viability:** Proper pH levels are critical for maintaining cell viability and function in cell culture. pH deviations outside the physiological range can lead to cell stress, metabolic disturbances, and ultimately cell death.

   b. **Cell Growth:** Optimal pH conditions are necessary for supporting cell growth, proliferation, and differentiation in culture. pH stability ensures that cells can undergo normal physiological processes and maintain their phenotype.

2. Buffering Systems in Cell Culture:

   a. **CO_2/Bicarbonate Buffer System:** In cell culture incubators, CO_2 gas is commonly supplied to maintain a stable pH in the growth medium through the bicarbonate buffer system. CO_2 dissolves in the medium, forming carbonic acid (H_2CO_3), which rapidly equilibrates with bicarbonate ions (HCO_3^-), thereby buffering changes in pH.

   b. **Phosphate Buffer System:** Phosphate buffers, such as phosphate-buffered saline (PBS), are commonly used in cell culture media to provide pH stability. Phosphate ions ($HPO_4^{2-}/H_2PO_4^-$) help maintain pH within the desired range, particularly in applications where CO_2 regulation may be insufficient.

3. Considerations for Buffering in Cell Culture:

a. **CO_2 Regulation:** CO_2 concentration in the cell culture incubator influences the pH of the medium through the CO_2/bicarbonate buffer system. Proper regulation of CO_2 levels ensures pH stability within the desired range.

b. **Medium Composition**: The composition of the cell culture medium, including buffering components, influences pH stability and cell growth. Buffered media formulations are available commercially or can be custom-prepared to meet specific pH requirements for different cell types and applications.

c. **pH Monitoring**: Regular monitoring of pH levels in the cell culture medium is essential to ensure pH stability and optimize cell growth conditions. pH meters or pH indicator dyes are commonly used to monitor and adjust pH as needed during cell culture experiments.

4. Buffering Capacity:

a. **Optimization:** Buffering capacity refers to the ability of a buffer system to resist changes in pH upon addition of acids or bases. Cell culture media are typically formulated with buffering components to provide adequate buffering capacity and maintain pH stability over the course of cell culture experiments.

b. **pH Range**: Buffering capacity should be optimized to maintain pH within the physiological range suitable for the specific cell type being cultured. This ensures that cells are exposed to optimal pH conditions for growth and function.

5. Applications in Cell Culture:

a. **Routine Cell Culture**: Buffering is essential for routine cell culture maintenance, ensuring pH stability and cell viability over extended culture periods.

b. **Cell-Based Assays**: Buffering is critical for maintaining consistent pH conditions during cell-based assays, where accurate measurement of cellular responses is dependent on stable pH environments.

c. **Bioproduction**: Buffering is important in large-scale bioproduction processes, such as the production of therapeutic proteins or monoclonal antibodies in bioreactors. Stable pH conditions are necessary for maximizing product yield and quality.

6. Challenges and Solutions:

a. **pH Drift**: pH drift, caused by metabolic activity or CO_2 fluctuations, can occur during prolonged cell culture. Regular monitoring and adjustment of CO_2 levels and buffer concentrations help mitigate pH drift and maintain pH stability.

b. **Media Formulation**: Selection of appropriate cell culture media and buffering components is essential for optimizing pH stability and cell growth. Custom media formulations may be required for specific cell types or applications to achieve optimal pH conditions.

BUFFERED ISOTONIC SOLUTIONS

Buffered isotonic solutions combine the properties of buffers and isotonic solutions to create a balanced environment for various biological and pharmaceutical applications. Here's a detailed overview of buffered isotonic solutions:

1. Definition:

Buffered Isotonic Solutions are aqueous solutions containing buffering agents and solutes adjusted to achieve isotonicity with physiological fluids. These solutions are formulated to maintain a stable pH while matching the osmotic pressure of bodily fluids, making them suitable for various medical, biological, and pharmaceutical applications.

Components:

1. Buffering Agents:

   a. Buffered isotonic solutions contain buffering agents, such as phosphate, bicarbonate, or citrate buffers. These buffers resist changes in pH by accepting or donating protons (H^+ ions) in response to acid or base additions.

2. Isotonic Solutes:

   a. Isotonic solutes, such as sodium chloride (NaCl) or glucose, are added to adjust the osmolarity of the solution. Isotonicity ensures that the solution has the same osmotic pressure as bodily fluids, preventing cellular swelling or shrinkage upon exposure.

Characteristics:

1. pH Stability:

   a. Buffered isotonic solutions maintain a stable pH level despite external influences, providing a controlled environment for biological and chemical processes.

2. Osmotic Balance:

   a. Isotonic solutes in the solution match the osmotic pressure of bodily fluids, preventing osmotic imbalances that could harm cells or tissues.

3. Biocompatibility:

   a. Buffered isotonic solutions are formulated to be biocompatible, minimizing adverse reactions or tissue damage when administered to living organisms.

Applications:

1. Medical Fluids:

a. Buffered isotonic solutions are used as intravenous fluids for hydration, electrolyte replenishment, and medication administration in clinical settings.

2. **Cell Culture Media:**

a. These solutions serve as basal media or supplements in cell culture applications, providing an optimal environment for cell growth and viability.

3. **Pharmaceutical Formulations:**

a. Buffered isotonic solutions are incorporated into pharmaceutical formulations, such as eye drops, nasal sprays, and injectable medications, to ensure compatibility with biological tissues and minimize irritation upon administration.

4. **Diagnostic and Therapeutic Procedures:**

a. They are utilized in various diagnostic tests and therapeutic procedures, such as wound irrigation and body cavity irrigation during surgical interventions.

Advantages:

1. **Safety:**

a. Buffered isotonic solutions reduce the risk of adverse reactions or tissue damage associated with solutions that are too acidic, too alkaline, or hypertonic.

2. **Biological Compatibility:**

a. These solutions closely mimic the composition and pH of bodily fluids, making them well-suited for biological and medical applications.

3. **Versatility:**

a. Buffered isotonic solutions can be tailored to specific pH ranges and osmolarities, allowing for customization based on the requirements of different applications and patient needs.

Components:

Buffered isotonic solutions are carefully formulated to provide both pH stability and osmotic balance, making them suitable for various biological and pharmaceutical applications. Here's a detailed look at the components of buffered isotonic solutions:

1. Buffering Agents:

Buffering agents are compounds that resist changes in pH by accepting or donating protons (H^+ ions) in response to acid or base additions. Common buffering agents used in buffered isotonic solutions include:

a. **Phosphate Buffers**: Phosphate salts, such as sodium phosphate and potassium phosphate, are commonly used buffering agents. Phosphate buffers are effective in the physiological pH range and are widely used in biological and medical applications.

b. **Bicarbonate Buffers**: Bicarbonate ions (HCO_3^-) and carbonic acid (H_2CO_3) form the bicarbonate buffer system, which plays a crucial role in regulating pH in the blood and extracellular fluids. Bicarbonate buffers are important components of buffered isotonic solutions for physiological compatibility.

c. **Citrate Buffers**: Citrate salts, such as sodium citrate and citric acid, can act as buffering agents over a wide pH range. Citrate buffers are often used in pharmaceutical formulations and diagnostic assays.

2. Isotonic Solutes:

Isotonic solutes are added to buffered solutions to adjust the osmolarity of the solution to match that of physiological fluids. Isotonicity ensures that the solution does not cause osmotic cell damage or excessive cell swelling/shrinkage. Common isotonic solutes include:

a. **Sodium Chloride (NaCl)**: Sodium chloride is the most commonly used isotonic solute. It is added to achieve an osmolarity similar to that of blood plasma, making it suitable for intravenous administration and other medical applications.

b. **Glucose**: Glucose is another isotonic solute commonly used in buffered isotonic solutions. It provides energy for cells and helps maintain osmotic balance in the solution.

3. Water:

Water is the solvent used to dissolve the buffering agents, isotonic solutes, and any other additives in the solution. It is essential for formulating solutions with the desired concentration and properties.

4. Additional Additives:

Depending on the specific application and formulation requirements, buffered isotonic solutions may contain additional additives such as:

a. **Preservative**s: Preservatives are added to prevent microbial growth and maintain the sterility of the solution, particularly in pharmaceutical formulations intended for multi-dose use.

b. **Stabilizers:** Stabilizers, such as antioxidants or chelating agents, may be included to protect the solution from degradation due to oxidation or metal ion catalysis.

c. **pH Adjusters:** In some cases, additional pH adjusters may be included to fine-tune the pH of the solution to the desired level.

d. **Excipients:** Excipients such as surfactants, viscosity modifiers, and flavoring agents may be added to improve the stability, palatability, or administration characteristics of the solution.

Characteristics:

Buffered isotonic solutions exhibit several key characteristics that make them suitable for a variety of biological, medical, and pharmaceutical applications. Here's a detailed look at the characteristics of buffered isotonic solutions:

1. pH Stability:

a. **Buffering Capacity**: Buffered isotonic solutions contain buffering agents that resist changes in pH, maintaining a stable pH level even when acids or bases are added.

b. **Optimal pH Range**: The buffering agents in these solutions are selected to operate within physiological pH ranges, ensuring compatibility with biological systems.

2. Osmotic Balance:

a. **Isotonicity**: Isotonic solutes in buffered solutions adjust the osmolarity to match that of physiological fluids, preventing osmotic cell damage and maintaining normal cell volume.

b. **Minimal Cellular Disruption**: Buffered isotonic solutions minimize the risk of cell swelling or shrinkage upon exposure, ensuring biocompatibility and cellular integrity.

3. Biocompatibility:

a. **Tissue Compatibility**: Buffered isotonic solutions are formulated to be biocompatible, minimizing tissue irritation, inflammation, or damage upon administration.

b. **Compatibility with Biological Fluids**: These solutions closely mimic the composition and properties of biological fluids, ensuring compatibility with biological systems.

4. Safety:

a. **Low Risk of Adverse Effects**: Buffered isotonic solutions are designed to be safe for use in medical, biological, and pharmaceutical applications, minimizing the risk of adverse reactions or tissue damage.

b. **Regulatory Compliance**: These solutions meet regulatory requirements for safety, quality, and efficacy in pharmaceutical and medical device applications.

5. Versatility:

a. **Application Flexibility**: Buffered isotonic solutions can be tailored to specific pH ranges, osmolarities, and compositions to meet the requirements of diverse applications and patient populations.

b. **Multiple Routes of Administration**: These solutions can be administered via various routes, including intravenous, intramuscular, oral, topical, and ophthalmic routes, depending on the intended use.

6. Stability:

a. **Physical and Chemical Stability**: Buffered isotonic solutions exhibit stability over a wide range of storage conditions, maintaining pH, osmolarity, and chemical composition over time.

b. **Long Shelf Life**: Properly formulated and packaged, these solutions have a long shelf life, ensuring product quality and consistency.

7. Compatibility:

a. **Compatibility with Excipients**: Buffered isotonic solutions are compatible with a wide range of excipients, allowing for the addition of preservatives, stabilizers, pH adjusters, and other additives as needed.

b. **Compatibility with Drug Formulations**: These solutions are compatible with a variety of drug substances and formulations, facilitating the development of pharmaceutical products for diverse therapeutic indications.

Applications:

Buffered isotonic solutions find diverse applications across various fields, including medicine, biotechnology, and pharmaceuticals, owing to their unique properties such as pH stability, osmotic balance, and biocompatibility. Here's a detailed exploration of their applications:

1. Medical Applications:

a. **Intravenous Fluids**: Buffered isotonic solutions, such as saline solutions (e.g., normal saline), are used for intravenous hydration, electrolyte replacement, and medication administration in hospitals and clinical settings.

b. **Wound Irrigation**: Buffered isotonic solutions are utilized for wound irrigation to clean and disinfect wounds, minimize infection risk, and promote healing without damaging healthy tissue.

c. **Ophthalmic Solutions**: Buffered isotonic solutions are employed as eye drops or irrigation solutions for rinsing and treating eye conditions, such as dry eyes, conjunctivitis, and corneal injuries.

d. **Nasal and Respiratory Care:** Buffered isotonic solutions are used as nasal sprays or nebulized solutions for nasal congestion relief, sinus irrigation, and respiratory care in conditions like allergies and sinusitis.

2. Biological Research:

a. **Cell Culture Media:** Buffered isotonic solutions serve as basal media or supplements in cell culture experiments, providing a stable pH environment and osmotic balance essential for cell growth, viability, and experimental reproducibility.

b. **In Vitro Assays**: These solutions are utilized in biochemical assays and in vitro experiments to maintain constant pH conditions, ensuring accurate measurement of enzyme kinetics, protein interactions, and other biological processes.

c. **Microbiology:** Buffered isotonic solutions are employed in microbiology laboratories for diluting and suspending microorganisms, preparing culture media, and conducting microbial assays and tests.

3. Pharmaceutical Formulations:

a. **Injectable Medications**: Buffered isotonic solutions are used as vehicles or diluents for injectable medications, ensuring compatibility, stability, and safety of the drug formulation during storage and administration.

b. **Topical Preparations**: Buffered isotonic solutions are incorporated into topical formulations, such as creams, gels, and lotions, to adjust pH, enhance solubility, and improve skin compatibility for dermatological applications.

c. **Nasal and Pulmonary Drug Delivery**: Buffered isotonic solutions are formulated as nasal sprays or inhalation solutions for drug delivery to the respiratory tract, treating conditions like asthma, chronic obstructive pulmonary disease (COPD), and nasal congestion.

4. Analytical Chemistry:

a. **pH Calibration Solutions**: Buffered isotonic solutions are used as standard reference solutions for calibrating pH meters and electrodes in analytical chemistry laboratories, ensuring accurate pH measurements in various samples and experiments.

b. **Titration Assays**: These solutions serve as titration buffers in acid-base titration assays, maintaining constant pH conditions for accurate determination of unknown concentrations of acids or bases.

5. Veterinary Medicine:

a. **Animal Healthcare**: Buffered isotonic solutions are utilized in veterinary medicine for hydration therapy, wound irrigation, and medication administration in animals, ensuring safe and effective treatment outcomes.

b. **Diagnostic Procedures**: These solutions are employed in diagnostic tests and procedures, such as sample collection, specimen preservation, and laboratory analyses, in veterinary clinics and research facilities.

Advantages:

Buffered isotonic solutions offer several advantages over other types of solutions, making them valuable components in various medical, biological, and pharmaceutical applications. Here's a detailed exploration of their advantages:

1. pH Stability:

a. **Buffering Capacity**: Buffered isotonic solutions contain buffering agents that resist changes in pH, ensuring a stable pH environment even when acids or bases are added. This stability is crucial for maintaining the integrity and functionality of biological systems and pharmaceutical formulations.

b. **Precise pH Control**: The buffering capacity of these solutions allows for precise control of pH levels within physiological ranges, ensuring optimal conditions for cell culture, enzymatic reactions, and other biological processes.

2. Osmotic Balance:

a. **Isotonicity**: Buffered isotonic solutions are formulated to have the same osmotic pressure as physiological fluids, preventing osmotic cell damage and maintaining normal cell volume. This isotonicity ensures compatibility with biological tissues and minimizes adverse reactions upon administration.

b. **Cellular Compatibility**: By maintaining osmotic balance, these solutions minimize cell swelling or shrinkage when exposed to the solution, preserving cellular integrity and function in biological and pharmaceutical applications.

3. Biocompatibility:

a. **Tissue Safety**: Buffered isotonic solutions are designed to be biocompatible, minimizing tissue irritation, inflammation, or damage upon administration. This ensures patient safety and comfort during medical procedures or pharmaceutical treatments.

b. **Compatibility with Biological Fluids**: These solutions closely mimic the composition and properties of biological fluids, ensuring compatibility with biological systems and minimizing adverse reactions or interactions.

4. Versatility:

a. **Application Flexibility**: Buffered isotonic solutions can be tailored to specific pH ranges, osmolarities, and compositions to meet the requirements of diverse applications and patient populations. This versatility allows for their use in a wide range of medical, biological, and pharmaceutical contexts.

b. **Multiple Routes of Administration**: These solutions can be administered via various routes, including intravenous, intramuscular, oral, topical, and ophthalmic routes, depending on the intended use. This flexibility enhances their applicability in different clinical and research settings.

5. Stability:

a. **Physical and Chemical Stability**: Buffered isotonic solutions exhibit stability over a wide range of storage conditions, maintaining pH, osmolarity, and chemical composition over time. This stability ensures product quality and consistency throughout their shelf life.

b. **Long Shelf Life:** Properly formulated and packaged, these solutions have a long shelf life, allowing for extended storage without degradation or loss of efficacy. This reduces waste and ensures availability when needed.

6. Safety:

a. **Low Risk of Adverse Effects**: Buffered isotonic solutions are safe for use in medical, biological, and pharmaceutical applications, minimizing the risk of adverse reactions or tissue damage. This enhances patient safety and ensures the effectiveness of treatments or procedures.

b. **Regulatory Compliance**: These solutions meet regulatory requirements for safety, quality, and efficacy in pharmaceutical and medical device applications. This compliance ensures their suitability for use in clinical settings and research laboratories.

Multiple-Choice Questions (MCQs)

1. What does pH stand for?

   A) Power of Hydrogen

B) Potential of Hydrogen

C) Potency of Hydrogen

D) Power of Hydration

2. Who introduced the concept of pH?

A) Albert Einstein

B) Isaac Newton

C) Søren Sørensen

D) Niels Bohr

3. What is the pH range of neutrality?

A) Less than 7

B) 7

C) More than 7

D) 0 to 14

4. What are buffers used for?

A) Increasing the pH of solutions

B) Decreasing the pH of solutions

C) Resisting changes in pH

D) Neutralizing acids only

5. Which type of buffer is made from acetic acid and sodium acetate?

A) Acidic Buffer

B) Basic Buffer

C) Neutral Buffer

D) Universal Buffer

6. What does an isotonic solution prevent?

A) Net movement of water across a cell membrane

B) Dissolution of solutes

C) Reaction between acids and bases

D) Increase in solute concentration

7. In which year was the pH scale introduced?

A) 1809

B) 1909

C) 2009

D) 1709

8. What is the typical pH range of human blood?

A) 6.35 to 6.45

B) 7.00 to 7.14

C) 7.35 to 7.45

D) 8.35 to 8.45

9. Which method of pH determination uses a glass electrode?

A) Electrometric

B) Colorimetric

C) Gravimetric

D) Volumetric

10. What does the color change in a colorimetric pH determination indicate?

A) Temperature change

B) Concentration of solutes

C) Change in pH

D) Change in pressure

11. Which buffer system is primary in blood?

A) Acetate Buffer

B) Phosphate Buffer

C) Bicarbonate Buffer

D) Tris Buffer

12. What is the Henderson-Hasselbalch equation used for?

A) Determining the osmolarity of a solution

B) Calculating the pH of a buffer solution

C) Measuring the volume of a solution

D) Determining the electrical conductivity of a buffer

13. What indicates a high buffer capacity?

    A) Low concentrations of weak acid and its conjugate base

    B) High concentrations of strong acid and strong base

    C) High concentrations of weak acid and its conjugate base

    D) Equal concentrations of strong acids and strong bases

14. What is the primary role of buffers in pharmaceutical formulations?

    A) Color enhancement

    B) Viscosity adjustment

    C) pH stability

    D) Scent improvement

15. What is the main purpose of using isotonic solutions in medical settings?

    A) To increase blood pressure

    B) To decrease blood pressure

    C) To maintain proper cell function

    D) To provide nutrients to cells

16. How does the phosphate buffer system function?

    A) It uses only strong acids

    B) It uses only strong bases

    C) It uses dihydrogen phosphate and hydrogen phosphate ions

    D) It uses carbonic acid exclusively

17. Which ions are involved in the regulation of blood pH through the bicarbonate buffer system?

    A) Na^+ and Cl^-

    B) K^+ and Cl^-

    C) HCO_3^- and H_2CO_3

    D) Ca^{2+} and Mg^{2+}

18. What type of buffer would likely be used in an enzyme study to maintain pH stability?

    A) Citrate buffer

B) Bicarbonate buffer

C) Tris buffer

D) Sulfate buffer

19. What is the effect of adding a strong base to an acidic buffer?

A) Decrease in pH

B) Increase in pH

C) No change in pH

D) Fluctuation in solute concentration

20. Which pH measurement method involves a color change due to protonation or deprotonation?

A) Electrometric

B) Gravimetric

C) Titrimetric

D) Colorimetric

Short Answer Type Questions

1. What is the definition of pH?
2. Explain how a buffer works to stabilize pH.
3. What is an isotonic solution?
4. Describe the significance of the pH scale introduced by Søren Sørensen.
5. What is the principle of electrometric pH determination?
6. How do colorimetric methods determine pH?
7. What role do buffers play in biological systems?
8. Explain the significance of isotonic solutions in medical settings.
9. What is the Henderson-Hasselbalch equation and what does it represent?
10. Describe the role of phosphate buffers in biological systems.
11. How do bicarbonate buffers regulate blood pH?
12. What is buffer capacity and why is it important?

13.Explain how changes in CO_2 levels affect blood pH.

14.Describe how pH is related to enzyme activity in biological systems.

15.What is the importance of buffers in pharmaceutical formulations?

16.Explain the relationship between pH and cellular signaling.

17.How does the bicarbonate buffer system function in extracellular fluids?

18.What is the difference between hypertonic and isotonic solutions?

19.Describe how buffering agents are selected for pharmaceutical use.

20.Explain the role of proteins as buffers in biological systems.

Long Answer Type Questions

1. Discuss the role of buffers in maintaining pH stability in biological systems and provide examples of where they are critically important.

2. Explain the principles and applications of electrometric methods for pH determination.

3. Describe the different methods available for measuring pH and their respective advantages and disadvantages.

4. Discuss the impact of pH on enzyme function and metabolism in human physiology.

5. Explain the relationship between buffer capacity and buffer composition, and how it affects the ability of a buffer to stabilize pH.

6. Describe the physiological mechanisms that regulate blood pH and the role of the bicarbonate buffer system in this process.

7. Discuss the applications and importance of isotonic solutions in medical treatments and cell culture.

8. Explain how buffers are used in pharmaceutical formulations to ensure drug stability and efficacy.

9. Describe the concept of buffer capacity, how it is calculated, and its significance in chemical and biological contexts.

10.Explain the interaction between respiratory and renal systems in maintaining acid-base balance in the human body.

Answer Key

1. (B) Potential of Hydrogen
2. (C) Søren Sørensen
3. (B) 7
4. (C) Resisting changes in pH
5. (A) Acidic Buffer
6. (A) Net movement of water across a cell membrane
7. (B) 1909
8. (C) 7.35 to 7.45
9. (A) Electrometric
10.(C) Change in pH
11.(C) Bicarbonate Buffer
12.(B) Calculating the pH of a buffer solution
13.(C) High concentrations of weak acid and its conjugate base
14.(C) pH stability
15.(C) To maintain proper cell function
16.(C) It uses dihydrogen phosphate and hydrogen phosphate ions
17.(C) HCO3- and H2CO3
18.(C) Tris buffer
19.(B) Increase in pH
20.(D) Colorimetric